D0407876

DIG DEEP

DIG DEEP

7 TRUTHS TO FINDING THE STRENGTH WITHIN

J. C. WATTS JR.

REGNERY
FAITH

Regnery Faith™ is a trademark of Salem Communications Holding Corporation; Regnery® is a registered trademark of Salem Communications Holding Corporation

Cataloging-in-Publication data on file with the Library of Congress

ISBN 978-1-62157-460-6   **33614056495582**

Published in the United States by
Regnery Faith
An imprint of Regnery Publishing
A Division of Salem Media Group
300 New Jersey Ave NW
Washington, DC 20001
www.RegneryFaith.com

Distributed to the trade by
Perseus Distribution
250 West 57th Street
New York, NY 10107

Manufactured in the United States of America

10 9 8 7 6 5 4 3 2 1

Books are available in quantity for promotional or premium use. For information on discounts and terms, please visit our website: www.Regnery.com.

To the memory of my parents, Buddy and Helen, who never allowed me to make my knuckleheadedness and dysfunctions my "normal," and to Frankie, my kids, my grandkids, and my siblings, who remind me that my family is the real wealth in my life.

CONTENTS

THE POWER OF DIGGING DEEP

"**S**uperhumanly determined." That's how *National Geographic* once described Reinhold Messner, a man it also dubbed "the world's greatest mountaineer."[1]

On May 8, 1978, Messner stood with his companion, Peter Habeler, at the summit of Mount Everest, the first men to climb the world's tallest peak without the use of supplemental oxygen. Even with the aid of oxygen and other sophisticated gear, the scaling of Everest is notoriously dangerous. More than 250 climbers have died in the attempt, the bodies of most of them lying on that mountain still.

Before Messner and Habeler impressed the world with their stunning achievement, most experts believed that summiting Everest without oxygen was impossible. Not even the local Sherpas of Nepal—legendary for their ability to operate in the dangerously thin air of the Himalayas—had done it. In fact, so "impossible" was this feat that many in Nepal refused to believe that Messner and Habeler had actually done what they claimed. Experienced climbers whispered to one another that they must have secretly carried small oxygen bottles in their gear.

Messner knew of the gossip and the lies, so two years later he decided to silence the doubters. In an epic ascent, he climbed Everest completely alone—the first man ever to do it—and did so without supplemental oxygen. It is almost impossible for those of us who aren't mountain climbers to fully grasp the difficulty of what this iron-willed hero pushed himself to accomplish.

In 1982 Messner wrote a book describing the grueling ordeal of his solo ascent. He described the agony of the final hours of the climb, when he would stagger a few yards, collapse, and then somehow summon the strength to get up again. "Once more I must pull myself together. I can scarcely go on. No despair, no happiness, no anxiety. I have not lost the mastery of my feelings, there are actually no more feelings. I consist only of will. After each few meters this too fizzles out in an unending tiredness. Then I think nothing, feel nothing. I let myself fall, just lie there. For an indefinite time I remain completely irresolute. Then I make a few steps again."[2]

Messner was able to accomplish what no other human being had ever accomplished because he had cultivated the ability to focus his will, to summon more inner strength than he even knew he possessed, and to put it to use. In other words, he had learned to dig deep.

Dig deep. This is the phrase I use for drilling into the core of who I am and drawing out the strength to achieve, the strength to fight another day. It means summoning the better version of J. C. Watts Jr. who lies within me and hurling him into the present battle. Digging deep is going beyond the excuses and the superficial reasons for failure and tapping inner reservoirs of inspiration, character, heritage, and motivation. I believe it is necessary for being the best we can be.

In fact, nearly every person who climbs to great heights of success, who lives an extraordinary life, has had to learn to dig deep. As Reinhold Messner taught us, the ability to dig deep is an essential skill for those who intend to stand upon the mountaintop.

Do you think you have this skill? If you don't have it now, do you think you can cultivate it? No? Well, I disagree! What if I can show you in these pages some of the keys to digging deep and living the rest of your days on this earth at a higher level? What if I can teach you how to be the best *you* possible? I believe you can do it. In fact, I believe you can do more, achieve more, and be more than you've ever dared to dream. Digging deep is the key. It is the skill most essential to real success in life and to becoming the best possible version of the person God created you to be.

I intend to show you how it is done.

You should understand from the start, though, that the type of success I have in mind isn't just about accumulating more prestige or greater possessions. True, these are sometimes the by-products of learning to dig deep. Yet wealth and fame alone do not make for real success. Our values teach us that, but so do the stories—which we hear almost every week—of the many fabulously wealthy people who take their own lives. News headlines constantly confirm that famous people are often chronically unhappy and routinely self-destructive. It seems the rich and famous need the kind of transformation I'm talking about just as desperately as the poor and obscure.

I know this is true because I have walked on both sides of the tracks. I have lived among the poor and obscure, and I have lived among the famous and successful. I am intimately familiar with the world of the "haves" and the world of the "have nots." This is why I can talk to you about how digging deep is essential for your success.

I was born in the small town of Eufaula in southeastern Oklahoma, a part of the state known as "Little Dixie." My father was the pastor of a Baptist church, a respected job that didn't pay much, so he had a second job as a police officer—the first black man in Eufaula to hold that position. He did a lot of other things as well, from cattle raising to entrepreneurial ventures of every kind. He did everything he could to make sure his family could eat.

Before I knew what the word *entrepreneur* meant, I witnessed the entrepreneurial spirit of J. C. Watts Sr. To my young eyes, entrepreneurship didn't look fancy or adventurous. It was working hard to put food on the table and a roof over the heads of your wife and children. I would never have used a word as sophisticated as *entrepreneur* to describe the sacrifices my father made every day. Years later I would learn that his entrepreneurial spirit lived in me. I was deeply grateful that he modeled a noble and productive life.

Even now I probably know only a small part of the price my father paid. I was born early enough in the twentieth century—in 1957, to be precise—to have personally seen the last vestiges of Jim Crow laws and attitudes, to have watched the struggles of the civil rights movement through wide young eyes. In fact, I was one of the first two black children to attend our local elementary school. It was named Jefferson Davis Elementary, after the president of the Confederacy. The only other local elementary school was named Dixie—not much better!

There was a reason our corner of Oklahoma had long been labeled Little Dixie. In many respects—culture, economy, attitudes, and politics—southeastern Oklahoma had more in common with rural Mississippi than with oil-rich Tulsa or the bustling western cow town Oklahoma City. My family had it better than some because of my father's hard work, but we escaped none of the bigotry directed at black families in those days.

Trust me, I know what it is to be despised, opposed, and obscure. Fortunately, I also know a bit about the lives of the rich and prominent. I've been rich only by the broadest definition of the word, but I have been privileged to achieve a remarkable level of success for someone who grew up as I did.

I've also had the opportunity to stand in the spotlight and hear the thunderous cheers of tens of thousands. Spotlights don't get much more intense than when you play quarterback for the University of Oklahoma Sooners, one of the most storied teams in all of college football. The pressure to perform and win at OU is extraordinary.

I was named the starter as a junior in the fall of 1979. Our coach, Barry Switzer, had built upon the rich legacies of his predecessor, Chuck Fairbanks, and the legendary Bud Wilkinson. In that proud, competitive culture, national championships and Heisman trophies were expected.

In my final two years at Oklahoma, we won back-to-back Big Eight Conference championships and achieved victories in two consecutive Orange Bowls. I was named our team's Most Valuable Player in both of those post-season wins. It was a thrilling time of my life, a time that built character, wisdom, and skill. It led to one of the great honors of my life—induction into the Oklahoma Sports Hall of Fame in 2014.

I experienced a different kind of spotlight and a different form of pressure when I became a U.S. congressman. My entry into politics came in 1990, when I was elected to the state Corporation Commission, the three-person body that regulates public utilities as well as the oil and gas industry, becoming the first black person of either party elected to statewide office in Oklahoma.

Five years later I ran for Congress in a district that hadn't sent a Republican to Washington since 1920. And I won. I'd be the first to admit I got more attention than I deserved because I was a black politician who wasn't a Democrat! Whatever the cause, I quickly began climbing through the ranks of the Republican leadership in Washington. One of the high points of my political career was delivering the Republican response to President Clinton's 1997 State of the Union address.

As grateful as I was for my political success, I had run on a promise not to make a career out of Congress, and after four terms I honored my pledge and simply walked away. I decided to try and contribute to the welfare of the country and tackle new challenges in the world of business. I trust there are even bigger business ventures to come in my life.

With all humility and gratitude, I can tell you I have been blessed with success in a number of arenas—athletics, ministry, politics, and business. Yet my success was no accident. It came about because I learned to dig deep, a lesson from the noble and hard-working lives of those who came before me. It was a treasure handed down and a legacy I now hope to pass on.

I think I can best do this by teaching what others have taught me about digging deep and by illustrating these truths with scenes from my own life. The experiences I share on the pages that follow are wholly mine. Please understand, though, the principles they illustrate—eternal, immutable truths woven into the fabric of the universe at the beginning of time—are for everyone. It is our privilege to discover them, to put them into practice, and to achieve more than we might ever have achieved before. We should always remember, though, that God is the author of these great and transforming realities.

There is a better life waiting for you. Its price is digging deep as I'm going to show you how to do. First, though, I want to challenge you to make a decision. Determine now that you are absolutely unwilling to remain as you are. Summon your hunger, your drive, your calling, and your passion to take hold of the best that God has destined you to be. Then accept the paradoxical truth that going higher in your life requires that you first dig deeper than you ever have before. If you determine that these are the new realities of your life, then as the Apostle Paul said, "nothing will be denied you."

Let's get started, then. The greater being God has destined you to be is waiting.

CHAPTER 1

THE ADVERSITY UPGRADE

*In the middle of every difficulty lies
an opportunity.*

—Albert Einstein

I t wasn't fair. It wasn't accurate. It wasn't right. But there it was, all the same.

My name—mentioned prominently in a sudden firestorm of media reports about a federal investigation into bribery and influence buying within the Oklahoma Corporation Commission, of which I had just become a member.

My face—next to headlines containing the words "FBI investigation," "corruption," and "scandal" in the big state newspapers and on local television newscasts. I'd had nothing to do with any of it. In fact, the wrongdoing under discussion had taken place long before I had even considered running for political office.

Nevertheless, my name was being publicly trashed and I couldn't for the life of me understand why.

Of course, I had been in politics for only two years and was something of a naïve rookie. In fact, I was so new to politics that I was still serving as the youth pastor at one of Oklahoma's many Baptist churches.

In other words, I was still relatively new to the self-interest-driven brutality of politics. Five years of NCAA Division I football and five years of professional football in Canada dodging massive defensive linemen had not prepared me for the violent blood sport of politics. Football I understood. It was played according to well-defined rules. You knew who your friends and your enemies were. The guys wearing the same color jersey as yours had your back. The guys wearing the other color were out to knock you down and make sure you failed. It was pretty straightforward.

Politics, as I was rapidly learning, was a much murkier game than football.

Allow me to back up a few steps and set the stage for what became the most grueling test of character I have ever endured. I share this story because it reveals some truths that can help you rise above adversity and unfair setbacks in your own life. There are few guarantees in life, but I can guarantee you this—and it isn't exactly good news: you *will* face adversity in the future. Life *will* be unfair at times. Yet you can transcend and even benefit from the cruelest of bad deals. As I once heard Bishop T. D. Jakes say, "Your adversity can become your advantage." He's right.

Here's what happened to me and how I was able to turn one of the worst seasons of my life into a life upgrade by digging deep. More important, here's how you can do the same.

I SOLEMNLY SWEAR

January 15, 1991, was a special day for me. It was the day I took the oaths of office as a freshly elected member of Oklahoma's three-person Corporation Commission. That's right, *oaths* of office—plural.

All elected officials in Oklahoma take a standard oath of office, vowing to uphold the state constitution and promising not to take money for performing their duties. Yet elected members of the Corporation Commission, who regulate Oklahoma's lucrative oil and gas industry as well as its public utilities, take an additional oath, unchanged since Oklahoma became a state in 1907. My right hand raised and my left hand resting on the Bible, a book I hold sacred and precious above all others, I repeated these words on that crisp January day:

> I, J. C. Watts, do solemnly swear that I am not, directly or indirectly, interested in any railroad, street railway, traction line, canal, steam boat, pipe line, car line, sleeping car line, car association, express line, telephone or telegraph line, nor in the bonds, stocks, mortgages, securities, contract or earnings of any railroad, street railway, traction line, canal, steam boat, pipe line, car

line, sleeping car line, car association, express
line, telephone or telegraph line; and that I will,
to the best of my ability, faithfully and justly
execute and enforce the provisions of this Constitution of the State of Oklahoma, and all the
laws of the State of Oklahoma concerning rail-
roads, street railways, traction lines, canals,
steam boats, pipe lines, car lines, sleeping car
lines, car associations, express lines, telephone
and telegraph lines, compress and elevator companies, and all other corporations over which said
Commission has jurisdiction.[1]

The language sounds archaic, but I meant every word.
My father, J. C. Watts Sr., had taught me that a man's word
is a sacred trust and one of his most precious possessions,
and the Bible upon which I'd rested my hand taught me that
"a good name is to be desired above great riches" (Prov.
22:1).

The final phrase of the commissioner's oath is the most
important today. Modern entities like telephone companies
and electrical power co-ops, which did not exist in 1907
but are now the focus of the commission's regulatory activity, are covered by "all other corporations over which said
Commission has jurisdiction."

Why a second oath, one not taken by any other state
officials? The framers of Oklahoma's constitution understood that the regulation of lucrative business interests is
fraught with moral peril. When tens or even hundreds of
millions of dollars are at stake for a telephone company or

an oil exploration firm in rulings by the Corporation Commission, the temptation to try to buy favors from officials can be strong. Many votes are decided by a two-to-one margin, moreover, making each commissioner a potential swing vote and therefore a tempting target for the unscrupulous.

As it turned out, the FBI and the U.S. attorney's office, completely unknown to me, had been investigating precisely this kind of corruption in Oklahoma for several years before I ran for the commission. Indeed, they would eventually indict, convict, and imprison a member of the commission, who resigned under a cloud a few months after I assumed office. I could not have imagined that I would be caught up in the scandal like a fallen leaf in a flood-swollen creek.

My swearing in was a heady yet sobering moment. My election in November 1990 was a major event for me personally, of course, but the first election of an African American to statewide office in Oklahoma was also a milestone for all black citizens of our state. The achievement meant a lot to my extended family back in eastern Oklahoma, the people of Eufaula, and the members of Sunnylane Baptist Church in Del City, an Oklahoma City suburb, where it had been my privilege to serve since retiring from professional football. It was particularly meaningful for the kids I ministered to each week as their youth pastor.

The national Republican Party leadership took notice as well, desperate to make electoral inroads into the black community and break the Democratic Party's near monopoly on its vote. They were also eager to diversify the uniformly white image that Republicans tended to present to the nation. Key persons inside the Beltway took note of the victory of a young, black Republican in a state that had been dominated by the Democrats for decades. In fact, about eighteen months after my election, my picture would appear on the front page of the state's largest newspaper, the *Daily Oklahoman*, standing beside President George H. W. Bush.

Looking back on it now, I'm sure all the national attention I received didn't sit well with Democrats and didn't exactly thrill some of my fellow Republicans in the state. Those with their own aspirations for higher office might have quietly resented this upstart who, in their view, hadn't paid the dues they had been paying. Believe me, I was far too politically naïve to have thought about that at the time. I simply set about fulfilling my new duties and approaching the new challenges and opportunities as I had done in my athletic career, doing my homework, showing up every day, working hard, and giving it my best. My experience taught me this was a formula for success.

Then, a few months after I had settled into my new job, one of my fellow commissioners suddenly retired even though he didn't have much time left in his term. Prior to being elected to the commission in 1986, he had served in the Oklahoma legislature for twenty-seven years. The governor appointed a replacement, Cody Graves, to finish out the balance of the retiring commissioner's term. At the time, I was puzzled by the commissioner's departure so close to the end of his term. Yet the reason for his exit would become clear the following year.

A PRONOUNCEMENT

I had served less than two years of my six-year term when, on Friday, October 2, 1992, all hell broke loose. One of the other commissioners, a Republican like me, came into my office with a serious expression on his face. "J. C.," he said, "I'm going to be making a big announcement today. I've been working with the FBI on something related to the commission." Then he added cryptically, "Note the dates I mention today. It will help you understand that this has nothing to do with you. Pay close attention to the dates."

Pay close attention to the dates? I couldn't imagine what he was talking about, but I didn't have to wait long to find out. A few minutes later, the commission convened in what is known as a "signing session."

An Oklahoma Corporation Commission meeting is essentially a court hearing in which the commissioners preside as judges. Sure enough, in the middle of the session, my colleague, who by virtue of seniority served as chairman of the commission, stopped the proceedings and said, "I have a pronouncement of the court to make."[2] *A pronouncement of the court?* This was unusual language to use in a matter the commissioners hadn't voted on. I questioned whether he had the authority to do it.

He went on to inform everyone present—including the handful of reporters assigned to cover the commission—that he had been cooperating with a federal investigation into corruption at the Oklahoma Corporation Commission since "before taking office in January of 1989." While working as a secret informant for the FBI, he had accepted "cash or inducement" from an official of the big regional telephone service provider.

He went on to suggest that there was evidence that "other commissioners" had engaged in "improper conduct." What he did *not* point out was that the other two sitting commissioners were new to the job and that the FBI's primary focus was the commissioner who had resigned the previous year. In other words, those "other commissioners" were no longer on the commission—a pretty important detail to leave out!

The following morning, Oklahoma City's business newspaper, the *Journal Record*, called these revelations "a bombshell." Indeed they were, sending shockwaves through the media and the government.[3] The disclosure had many legal and political experts scratching their heads, wondering why this commissioner, if he was part of an ongoing undercover probe, was revealing it to the public before any indictments had been handed down. And why was *he* making the announcement rather than the U.S. attorney's office? There was speculation that my colleague was trying to jumpstart his floundering campaign for Congress roughly thirty days before the election.[4] It was baffling—and fascinating.

Whatever his reasons, my colleague's vague but incendiary announcement threatened my reputation and that of every other employee of the commission. A few weeks later, he poured gasoline on that fire.

"CRISIS AT THE COMMISSION"

In the seventy-two hours following the Friday bombshell, I got my first up-close-and-personal look at a media feeding frenzy—at least one that wasn't about football. The statement by the chairman of the Corporation Commission—"There is evidence that one or more commissioners were involved in improper conduct, and I have given this evidence to the FBI"[5]—made it clear that there was blood in the water, but *whose* blood was unclear.

Throughout that weekend and into the following Monday, media speculation ran wild about who at the commission might be under investigation. Every news report named Cody Graves and me as the other two sitting commissioners. Of course, I had no way of knowing whether I was under investigation. All I knew was that I hadn't done anything wrong.

It didn't help that the FBI and the U.S. attorney weren't answering press questions about the ongoing investigation, letting the media conjecture machine continue to spin. Finally, on Tuesday, the chairman of the commission, on the campaign trail for a seat in Congress, held a news conference to answer questions about his shocking earlier statement.

He was asked point-blank who the focus of the FBI's investigation was and if any current commissioners were targets. His answer started out generally helpful: "Largely, the things that I referenced in my statement, I think, reference my first two years in office."[6] So far so good. Events would ultimately show that this was indeed the case. The focus of the investigation centered around events before either Cody Graves or I sat on the commission.

The chairman could not leave the matter there, though. Having already muddied his statement with the qualifying words "largely" and "I think," he added, "However, I'm not able to give anybody at the commission a clean bill of health."[7] He suggested that reporters ask me and Graves directly if we had done anything improper. "I don't office with those people," he said. "I don't travel with people on a minute-by-minute basis, and I can't speak for the other people."[8]

So while my colleague did confirm that the focus of the investigation was on actions that occurred before either of us other commissioners had assumed office, the only words some in the media seemed to hear were, "I'm not able to give anybody at the commission a clean bill of health." The front-page headline of the next morning's *Daily Oklahoman* shouted: "Chairman Won't Exonerate His Fellow Commissioners."[9]

It was on. I had thought the previous days had been insane, but the true insanity was just beginning. The story was all the local talk radio hosts gabbed about from then on, their call-in lines lit up like Times Square. One local television station branded its ongoing coverage "Crisis at the Commission."

What I couldn't have imagined at the time was that this ugly circus would continue for months. Drip, drip, drip—it was like Chinese water torture. Every few days some new development would bring the story back to the forefront of the news. And each time, my name and my face appeared, but no facts. Just speculation, suspicion, and innuendo.

I eventually went to the source to get some answers. Speaking to the FBI's local office, I asked directly, "Am I in any way a focus of this investigation that everyone is talking about?" The answer I received, from someone in a position to know, was clear and unequivocal: "No. We have no interest in you, Mr. Watts." He went on to say that I could tell the press what he had told me, but if the press called the FBI to confirm, the response would be neither confirmation nor denial.

It was maddening. Toward the end of the ordeal, I was able to speak with acting U.S. Attorney John Green, a truly decent man and honorable public servant, who told me, "We never had any interest in you, J. C. We didn't mean for your name to be dragged through the mud." Yet that's precisely what was happening. And the mud dragging got worse.

The association of my name with this mess was an incentive for the media to start digging around in my past—and not everyone doing the digging was on my side. I wore quite a collection of polarizing labels: Black, Republican, Conservative, and Evangelical Christian. It's a sad reality of life in this fallen world that some people had a problem with me simply because I was black. A lot of black folks had a problem with me because I was a Republican. Many Democrats were incensed that I had dared to wander off the reservation and stubbornly chose to think for myself. In the minds of some, you stop being authentically black the moment you depart from liberal orthodoxy.

It wasn't hard to discover that I had experienced some financial setbacks as a young man in the early 1980s. I graduated from the University of Oklahoma in 1981 and began playing professional football in Canada that year. Though the salaries there didn't compare to those in the

NFL, I was making real money for the first time in my life, and I invested it in a variety of ventures in my home state, including real estate and oil and gas exploration.

The history books now tell a story I couldn't have known at the time. The price of oil was about to plunge, triggering a financial earthquake in Oklahoma that would eventually bring down the Penn Square Bank and precipitate a severe and long-lasting regional recession. I took a big hit in the ensuing fallout. So did a lot of other people. In fact, a huge wave of bankruptcies swept the state in the early and mid-1980s. Fortunately, I was not one of them. I understand why some people file for bankruptcy, and there is a reason the law provides that option, but though I was a young man with a mountain of obligations, I just couldn't take that road. My father had taught me that if you take on a financial obligation, you do everything you legally and ethically can to satisfy it. You don't just walk away. I did everything I could to make my creditors whole, but it got ugly for a few years. It would have been much quicker, cleaner, and far less painful to file for bankruptcy and start fresh. Yet I believed in my heart that was the wrong path for me. It was a matter of principle. Now, a decade later, the media were going over that chapter of my life with a fine-tooth comb.

The Corporation Commission circus rolled on in increasingly ridiculous but embarrassing ways. At one of the low points, a television station sent an investigative reporter and cameraman to question Jerry Don Abernathy, the senior pastor of the church where I was the youth pastor, assuring him that his answers would not be filmed. They lied. The camera was laid on the floor, rolling, capturing the whole interview.

On the news that night was the pastor of Sunnylane Baptist Church, a prince of a man, filmed from a cockroach's perspective, answering questions about whether the church was taking money from the utilities to help pay J. C. Watts's salary. His answer was, "No. Absolutely not." But the stealthy way the story was shot and narrated gave the piece a seedy, sinister feel that was wildly unfair. My pastor was gracious about it afterward, but I was deeply grieved. It was bad enough that this defiling carnival sideshow oozed into every corner of my life as a public servant. Now it spilled over into my life as a youth minister.

It wouldn't be the last time. Nine months after the story first erupted, it was still a regular feature in the papers and on the evening news. For example, a report in the *Daily Oklahoman* on June 24, 1993, revealed that when I was running for office in 1990, my name had been loosely and repeatedly used without my knowledge by the chairman of the Corporation Commission—working on behalf of the FBI—to bait the utilities into offering illegal campaign cash. These new revelations about the investigation further and forever linked my name to a scandal I had no part in and knew nothing about.

While I was going about my business running for the commission, the "undercover" commissioner, working on behalf of the FBI, was soliciting large campaign donations, pretending they were for me, attempting to find out if a certain utility representative could be induced to pay bribes. It turned out he could. The bigger problem for me was that the utilities representative gave a large amount of cash to the chairman in the belief the money was being passed on to me. Of course, the money was turned over to the FBI as evidence, but my name had been used as bait, and all without my knowledge.

Naturally, I never saw any of that money, nor did I know my name was being used to obtain it. Yet here I was having to answer reporters' questions about it. Furthermore, I knew without a doubt that if any questionable contributions had come my way, I would have either refused them or reported them. Yet that wasn't an assumption the commentators were making.

A long, complex, and confusing article in the *Daily Oklahoman*—so confusing that it easily could have left the casual reader with the impression that I was somehow involved in the mess—ended by noting, "Watts is scheduled to be ordained as a Baptist minister Sunday. He will become associate pastor in addition to youth minister at Sunnylane Southern Baptist Church in Del City."[10] Once again, my church and ministry were dragged into the muck of politics at its worst.

I was indeed ordained that weekend. Before the ceremony, in which the deacons of the church and other ministers gather around the candidate, lay their hands upon him, and pray, someone quipped that maybe they should be praying for me concerning my *other* job. We all laughed, but there was a sobering element of truth at the heart of the joke. I needed all the prayer support I could get.

Of course, my wife and I did a lot of praying ourselves. I consistently cried out to God for lots of things—help, strength, vindication, and restoration in particular. Anything good He cared to send my way, I was wide open to receive. I was grateful for all the help I could get, for in the midst of all that chaos, I may have occasionally lost sight of an important truth I once heard a preacher draw out of the immense riches of the 103rd Psalm. The sixth and seventh verses of this classic psalm of David declare:

> The Lord executes righteousness
> And justice for all who are oppressed.
> He made known His *ways* to Moses,
> His *acts* to the children of Israel.[11]

In that hard season, I would have been drawn to the first of those two verses, the one in which God promises to look after the oppressed. I certainly felt unjustly oppressed. But it was the next verse that actually held the key to my troubles. Moses had a closer, more intimate relationship with God than did the rank-and-file children of Israel. They had seen God's wondrous "acts." But Moses was acquainted with His "ways"—something far more important and precious.

When we're slogging through hard times, we want to see God's acts, but He's often trying to teach us His ways. I wanted my problem to go away. God wanted to use my problems as an opportunity to reveal something to me about myself.

And that is precisely what He did.

IT'S NOT WHAT THEY DID *TO* ME.
IT'S WHAT THEY DID *FOR* ME.

The things that were said about me in the Corporation Commission scandal weren't accurate, and what happened to me wasn't fair. But life isn't always fair, and I don't intend to throw a pity party here. I'm not looking for sympathy. I'm looking to help you.

You see, although this season of my life was unbelievably frustrating and hard, I came through it. In fact, I came through it stronger, wiser, and with an enlarged capacity to lead, love, and live. I learned things. I grew. Looking back, I choose not to view this experience as something that was done *to* me. Rather I've come to view it as something that was done *for* me. I don't think I would have accomplished half of what I've done over the past twenty years without that trial and testing. It prepared me to walk in my destiny.

There is a remarkable moment in the Old Testament account of the life of Joseph. As we read in the book of Genesis, years after his jealous and embittered half-brothers had sold him into slavery and broken their father's heart, Joseph encountered them once again. Yet he didn't greet them with vindictiveness or anger. He restored them to his fellowship and said something extraordinarily wise and insightful: "You intended to harm me, but God intended it for good to accomplish what is now being done, the saving of many lives."[12]

Henry Ford had something like that in mind when he said, "Life is a series of experiences, each one of which makes us bigger, even though sometimes it is hard to realize this. For the world was built to develop character, and we must learn that the setbacks and grief which we endure help us in our marching onward."

Unfortunately, I've discovered that not every person reaps the benefits of adversity. Some, instead of rising above it, sink into the quicksand of bitterness and never find a way out. I witnessed this many times in sports. A brilliant player makes a key mistake at a crucial moment of a vital game, costing his team a win. Some players are able to learn from such a mistake and build on it, actually becoming better in pressure situations afterward. Others are never the same. It gets in their heads, undermining their confidence and making them indecisive in critical moments.

You have almost certainly seen this play out in heartbreaking ways in a contest with much higher stakes—the game of life. For example, the loss of a child is one of the most devastating things parents can face. Some couples come through this awful storm with a tighter and stronger relationship, but often the loss wrecks the marriage, the searing pain opening a chasm between the grieving parents that they never find a way to bridge. I've seen it happen more than once.

What makes the difference? Why does one person come through a major crisis stronger and better while another emerges broken and defeated, sometimes never to rise again? Looking back, I see five key attributes—habits or practices—that enabled me to turn adversity to advantage. As a lifelong student of achievement and leadership, I've seen them in the lives of many others for whom hard times or tragedy became not an anchor holding them back but a springboard launching them farther and higher than ever.

They're not gifts you're born with. They're not talents or personality traits. They are choices. I repeat, they are *choices*. You can choose to make these attributes part of who you are and how you live. They are learned responses that can be cultivated in the heart and mind of any person.

1. REJECT BITTERNESS AND SELF-PITY

"I can't catch a break."

"It's like the whole world has it out for me."

"Everything that can go wrong, has gone wrong."

"I hate those people, and I'm going to pay them back some day."

When you've been "done wrong," it is the most natural thing in this fallen world to drink deeply and often from the cup of bitterness. It tastes good. It can become our comfort food in hard times. It feels appropriate in the moment. You think you've earned that drink, but you'll find that bitterness is a poison that taints the soul.

In 1923, B. C. Forbes, the founder of *Forbes* magazine, wrote, "Self-pity is self-destruction. Self-pity breeds despair. It hurts self and it disgusts others."[13] I once heard the Bible teacher Joyce Meyer say that harboring bitterness against a person who has wronged you is like taking poison and hoping your enemy will die. Martin Luther King said, "Never succumb to the temptation of bitterness," and he called hate "too great a burden to bear." In a Fourth of July sermon in 1965, he warned, "I've seen hate. Hate distorts the personality. Hate does something to the soul that causes one to lose his objectivity. The man who hates can't think straight;

the man who hates can't reason right; the man who hates can't see right; the man who hates can't walk right."[14]

There were certainly many moments throughout my ordeal in which I sipped from that cup, tempted to cry, "Bottom's up!" But several things kept me from doing so.

First of all, I had been taught better—by my parents, by wise pastors, by coaches, and by many mentors through the years. On more than one occasion as I was growing up, I'd been grabbed by the scruff of the neck (figuratively) in the middle of a pity party and exhorted to suck it up, stay positive, and press through.

Furthermore, I knew I had an example to set. Over the years as a youth pastor I had tried to teach my kids that it's important to trust God when faced with life's challenges. I'd also encouraged them to understand the power of being "others-focused" rather than "self-absorbed"—to realize that no matter how rough things seem, there are always people enduring much worse. I taught them that if you just keep putting God and others first, God will take care of you.

I remember many times looking at myself in the mirror when I was really hurting and saying, "J. C., this is an opportunity to live what you believe. It's time to turn theory into practice." And that is precisely what I resolved in my heart to do. That was my game plan. Of course, my execution of that plan was imperfect. Some days my words and actions matched my ideals more closely than others. I'm sure I muttered some things I shouldn't have. Even so, all of these things worked together to keep me from sliding too far down the slippery slope of bitterness. I'm grateful they did.

When you suffer pain or loss because of the actions of another person, there is a powerful temptation to adopt "victim" as your identity. It's natural, and we have all done it. It's possible to wear your loss and the injustice you've suffered like a Purple Heart.

How does this happen? Gradually. When you've been wronged, you tend to get a lot of sympathy from people around you. This attention can become habit forming. The fact is, it's possible to invest so much of yourself in your victimhood and your claim on the sympathy of others that you lose sight of who you are without these artificial props.

I've encountered a few people in my life who have gotten stuck in this way. They progressively come to believe they have value only in the light of a wrong that was done to them. Their victimhood becomes a ready excuse for every failing, a "Get Out of Jail Free" card they produce as needed. I'm not minimizing what happened to these people. Each one experienced truly crushing things in his or her life, but God has so much more in store for them beyond the cul-de-sac of self-pity. There is more He wants to do in them and, more importantly, *through* them.

When you're going through something awful, the pain isn't optional. If it hurts, it hurts. Yet succumbing to the poison of bitterness is a choice. Refusing to drink deeply of that cup is the first step to turning adversity into advancement.

2. TRUST IN GOD'S GOODNESS

The Twenty-seventh Psalm is an amazing piece of poetry authored by the future king of Israel, David, when everything seemed to be going against him. He was running for his life from the soldiers and bounty hunters of a deranged king. Accused of things he hadn't done, he was pursued like a dog from cave to cave, lonely, homesick, and in daily fear for his life. In this dark season, David penned a beautiful song affirming his trust in God and in his eventual vindication, a song that ends,

> I would have despaired unless I had believed that
> I would see the goodness of the Lord in the
> land of the living.
> Wait for the Lord; Be strong and let your heart
> take courage;
> Yes, wait for the Lord.[15]

My situation was never nearly as grim as David's, yet I understand exactly the heartbeat of this psalm. An anchor for my soul through every storm of life has been a deep-rooted belief that a good God sees me, knows me, and is providentially active in the world. I've come to believe that no matter what I go through, I too will see "the goodness of the Lord in the land of the living." I can testify from personal experience that this belief is a mighty defense against the highest waves of despair.

I vividly recall an interview I gave to a reporter at the craziest, most hurtful point of my ordeal, when my reputation was being unjustly tarnished, and when my wife and

kids were upset by seeing my name associated with a bribery scandal on the news almost every night. I was asked for
my reaction to rumors that I was the focus of an FBI investigation. Of course, I would later learn those rumors were
false, but I didn't know that at that moment. My sincere
reply was, "I honestly don't understand all that is going on,
but I will cooperate completely and await the results in
peace." I meant every word.

It was my Psalm 27 stand. Although I was frequently
agitated and upset at the surface level, in the deepest part
of me I really did have a profound sense of peace. That
peace was not born of confidence in myself. I knew myself
better than that. Nor was it a product of any confidence I
had in the justice system. Far from it. My trust in our system
of justice was shaken and was getting shakier by the
moment. No, my confidence was in a sovereign God Who,
by His grace and mercy, had made me His son. My trust
was in Him.

The competitor in me wanted to fight back, to body
slam some folks, to find a way to "win" this battle, but
there was nothing I could do. For each one of us on the
journey of life, there comes a point at which all he can do
is stand still and trust God. That requires trust and a healthy
dose of humility.

I like what Joyce Meyer once said along these lines:
"The humble person is quick to forgive, difficult to offend
and glad to wait on God for vindication."[16] Part of the work
God was doing in me through this fiery trial was teaching
me humility.

3. MAINTAIN A HEART OF GRATITUDE

It was a Sunday morning, and to be honest, I didn't really feel like singing, but out of lifelong practice I was in church. In fact, it was my job to be there. I was the youth pastor, after all.

My mind was elsewhere, my mood on the sour side. Those first weeks of the media circus surrounding the commission had left me distracted, discouraged, and feeling persecuted. However hard I tried to focus on the church service, my mind kept snapping back to my problems. If you had asked me at that moment how things were going, my gut-honest answer would probably have been, "Everything stinks. And I mean *everything*."

Then I heard Kendal Lucas, our cheery music minister, say, "Let's stand and sing hymn number 644, 'Count Your Blessings!'" I may have groaned a little on the inside—at least I hope it was on the inside. Not only did I not feel like singing, I especially didn't feel like singing *that*. Something like hymn number 149, "Jesus Knows Thy Sorrow," would have been a better fit with my mood, or maybe number 410, "It Is Well with My Soul," with its line about sorrows rolling like sea-billows. But that wasn't the play the quarterback called, so like any good teammate, I rose to my feet to give it my best. *Baptist Hymnal* in hand, I plunged into the first verse:

> When upon life's billows you are tempest tossed,
> When you are discouraged, thinking all is lost,
> Count your many blessings, name them one by
> one,

And it will surprise you what the Lord hath
done.[17]

"Well, okay," I admitted to myself. "Maybe this song is
a little more relevant than I first assumed." After the chorus,
we're on to the second verse, and then the third:

So, amid the conflict, whether great or small,
Do not be discouraged, God is over all;
Count your many blessings, angels will attend,
Help and comfort give you to your journey's
end.[18]

What timely advice this song carried. As I sang, I
couldn't help but recall that I really did have so very much
to be grateful for. I had a wife and kids who were better
than I deserved. I also had a couple of real friends. Pat
Adams, Gary Moores, Danny Kirby, Mike Jones, Paul Ray
Dixon, Rusty Griffis, and others knew me before I was a
commissioner or OU quarterback and were deeply committed to me. At that very moment, loving and supportive
people filled the pews all around me. A funny thing happened somewhere between the second chorus and the third
verse. The more I turned my attention to things for which
I could be grateful, the more of them came to mind.

All our material needs were met. My kids had a roof
over their heads, plenty to eat, and two committed parents
watching over them. In the weeks preceding this service, I
had been deeply saddened by images and reports coming
out of Somalia that depicted what came to be known as the

"first humanitarian war." The battle of Mogadishu—portions of which would eventually be depicted with heartbreaking realism in the movie *Blackhawk Down*—was only months away. Largely forgotten now, that war was one of the worst human-caused crises of my lifetime. When I contrasted the prospects of those Somali children with those of my kids, my heart almost burst with gratitude for how privileged we were.

As so often happens when you show up at church, I heard exactly what I needed to hear. Through the music minister, God had written the perfect prescription for my ailing soul. I needed a change of perspective, to shift my focus. I was allowing my problems and challenges to loom so large that they threatened to crowd out my view of the good in my life.

It's a fact of human nature that dwelling on the negative rather than the positive eventually affects the way you view everything in your life, and your gloomy outlook becomes a self-fulfilling prophecy. King Solomon wrote, "As a man thinks in his heart, so is he." Positive thinking is more than just a slogan. I've never known teammates to follow a quarterback who gets in the huddle and says, "I don't know if we're good enough to beat these guys." No, they're looking for someone that believes they can win and says, "We can and we *will* beat these guys."

If you know anything about cognitive biases—the quirky ways in which our brains can cloud our judgment and distort the way we perceive reality—then you're probably familiar with the most common of these, *confirmation bias*. It's our tendency to notice the things that conform to what we *expect* to see and not to notice the things we *don't* expect to see. Put another way, when we believe something to be true, we take special note of things that validate that belief. At the same time, we're blind to things that don't fit our beliefs.

This feature of human nature is powerfully in play when gratitude is competing with gloominess. We see what we're looking for. If you're looking for problems, you'll see problems everywhere. If you believe you can't catch a break and everyone—including God—is out to get you, then you're going to notice everything that seems to validate that belief and be blind to a hundred blessings.

In the same way, if you're looking for things to be thankful for—if you believe in your heart that God will reward you in the long run for doing the right thing—you're going to notice evidence of those things all around you. They would have been there either way. It's just that your attitude attuned your brain to *see* them.

Dwelling on the negative even affects your body. A growing number of studies have revealed that maintaining a heart of gratitude and a positive outlook brings huge physical benefits. For example, researchers had a group of people keep a daily "gratitude journal," in which they simply wrote down things for which they were grateful. Compared with the control group, the gratitude group reported:

- 16 percent fewer symptoms of illness
- 19 percent more time spent exercising
- 10 percent less physical pain
- 8 percent more sleep
- 25 percent increased quality of sleep.[19]

Facts are facts. Study after study has shown that positive people are healthier, less stressed, and generally happier. Chronically grateful people report that they spend less time feeling sick and more time feeling better about their lives, and they're optimistic about the future.[20]

I'm not talking about being in denial about your problems, putting your head in the sand and pretending everything is perfect and sunny when it isn't. I'm talking about making sure you don't let your very real challenges become the only things you see, making sure you protect yourself from slipping into a self-reinforcing negativity spiral that darkens your heart.

John Piper calls thankfulness "an essential guardian of the soul" and encourages us to "guard ourselves with gratitude."[21] It's possible to cultivate a lifestyle of gratitude that permeates every aspect of your life. It's what G. K. Chesterton had in mind when he wrote, "You say grace before meals. All right. But I say grace before the concert and the opera, and grace before the play and pantomime, and grace before I open a book, and grace before sketching, painting, swimming, fencing, boxing, walking, playing, dancing and grace before I dip the pen in the ink."[22]

Few practices are more powerful and important when you're moving through a hard season. And that's the point—to move "through" that season and come out the other side. As Winston Churchill once said, "When you're going through hell, keep going." Which brings me to the next of my five key attributes for turning adversity into advancement.

4. CULTIVATE A SPIRIT OF DETERMINATION

Ancient Greek athletic contests often featured a foot race in which each runner carried a torch, the prize going not to the man who crossed the finish line first, but to the first man to cross with his torch still burning, a race we commemorate when a runner bearing a torch enters the stadium to open the modern Olympic games.

The race you and I are running is a lot like that. It's not just about getting from point A to point B in the shortest possible time. Shortcuts and cheating won't produce real victory. You and I are charged with running the race of life in such a way that the torch of integrity and character is still burning when we get to the end, in spite of our messes, stumbles, setbacks, and heartaches.

"You have need of endurance," the apostle wrote to the Hebrews, "so that after you have done the will of God, you may receive the promise."[23] In a similar vein, Paul told the Corinthians: "Don't you realize that in a race everyone runs, but only one person gets the prize? So run to win! All athletes are disciplined in their training. They do it to win a prize that will fade away, but we do it for an eternal prize. So I run with purpose in every step."[24]

It's no accident that Paul's writing is filled with references to athletic contests, for success in sports and success in life both require what the epistle to the Hebrews calls endurance. It's a quality that goes by a variety of names. I tend to call it determination, but I've heard it called grit, persistence, perseverance, and occasionally an old-fashioned, hardheaded refusal to quit. Whatever you call it, it's indispensable if you're going to come through a season of trouble, setbacks, or adversity.

"Nothing in the world can take the place of persistence," said President Calvin Coolidge. "Talent will not; nothing is more common than unsuccessful men with talent. Genius will not; unrewarded genius is almost a proverb. Education will not; the world is full of educated derelicts. Persistence and determination alone are omnipotent."

I learned the power and importance of determination in my years in competitive athletics. I boxed and played football and basketball, learning to play through injuries, to ignore distractions, and when utterly exhausted, to draw on reserves I didn't know I possessed. I needed every ounce of determination I had acquired as I pressed through my ordeal on the Corporation Commission. You'll need plenty of determination for your hard season or setback as well.

Stubborn determination isn't glamorous. Grit isn't sexy. But like Calvin Coolidge, I've discovered that this quality is more common in winners than talent or genius. I'm convinced that I owed my own success in football much more to determination than to talent. I was rarely the fastest, the strongest, or the biggest, but I rarely competed against someone with more determination. Maybe being the fifth of six children gave me a head start on cultivating tenacity.

A lot of people, fired up and filled with energy, talk a good game in the pre-game warm-ups, but it's in the fourth quarter, when grit and guts count more than chatter, that games are won or lost. Every year I played football at the University of Oklahoma, we knew before the season started that the race for the Big Eight Conference championship would come down to us and Nebraska, and I would have to call on everything I had to beat the Cornhuskers in the fourth quarter. And I did!

The German writer Johann von Goethe seemed to have this fourth-quarter reality in mind when he wrote, "In the realm of ideas, everything depends on enthusiasm; in the real world, all rests on perseverance."[25] Thomas Edison endured countless failures in his search for a workable filament for his electric light bulb, but he simply refused to quit trying. Later he would say, "I didn't fail a thousand times. I simply discovered a thousand ways it won't work." Regarding the power of determination, he once told a reporter, "The first requisite for success is to develop the ability to focus and apply your mental and physical energies to the problem at hand—without growing weary.... Many of life's failures are experienced by people who did not realize how close they were to success when they gave up." In other words, don't quit, don't quit, and don't quit. You can do it.

Determination is the power to finish, but it doesn't have to be just "grim determination." That brings me to my fifth and final key to turning your setback into a springboard.

5. LAUGH

A "man's man" with a girl's name, Faye Odell had a profound influence on me early in my life as a public speaker and as a Christian. When we first met, I was a young college athlete and he was one of the Fellowship of Christian Athletes' most sought-after speakers. I also spoke on the FCA circuit when my schedule permitted.

A gifted, multi-sport high school athlete in the early 1940s, Faye left a full football scholarship at the University of Arkansas to join the Marine Corps and fight in the Pacific theater in the waning days of World War II. He resumed his studies and athletics at what is now the University of Central Oklahoma, returning to war—this time in Korea—a few years after graduating.

A high school coaching legend in Oklahoma in the 1950s and '60s, Faye had a long and celebrated second career as a motivational speaker, his inspiring talks about God, country, and service to others becoming FCA favorites. His death in 2007 triggered an outpouring of tributes from people around the nation whose lives he'd touched.

A hallmark of Faye's popular, life-changing talks was humor, and this athletic, battle-hardened Marine was hilarious one-on-one as well. He liked to say to me, "What if my parents had named me Julius Caesar and your parents had named you Faye? How different would our lives have been?" He had my sides aching as he explored that alternative reality with his fertile imagination and wit. He liked to share his coach's secret for quickly determining how seriously injured a downed player really was. He would kneel down beside the player and whisper, "You'd better get up. Your mother's heading out onto the field." If that didn't get the young man off the turf quickly, he was probably really hurt.

Bringing his audience to a crescendo of hilarity, Faye would deliver a deep and biblical truth about how vital laughter is for the human soul, often quoting Proverbs 17:22: "A merry heart does good, like medicine, but a broken spirit dries the bones."[26] I have always tried to be positive and optimistic. My father and his brothers, my Uncles Wade and Lois, a reliable presence and influence in my upbringing—filled our house with their laughter and had a knack for making others laugh as well.

So when my wife and I began to make our way through the bewildering and humiliating labyrinth of the Corporation Commission scandal, it was natural for us to resort to humor to lighten the heavy atmosphere. It was hard sometimes, but the ability to laugh at ourselves and at the absurdity of our circumstances was an indispensable source of strength and light for us in the darkest of those days.

Laughter really is medicine for our souls. And we need it today more than ever. How did our culture become so grim and angry? I know the twenty-four-hour news cycle and ideologically driven cable news contribute. It's not difficult to watch current affairs shows every day and think, "There's no joy in us." Everyone seems to be mad about something. Of course, no one watches those cable shout-fests to learn something new. We watch to have someone validate what we already think, which only makes us angrier.

I suspect that the rise of social media, however, has intensified this perpetual outrage. Platforms like Facebook and Twitter allow us to further insulate ourselves from perspectives different from our own. They feed our outrage 24/7. That constant drip of bad news and offense quickly colors our perception of the world we live in: *The country is going to hell in a hand-basket. Everything is horrible. The bad guys are on the rise everywhere. The good guys are under siege everywhere. Nothing is good or right or fair or just.*

I know one family that split into two camps and engaged in a shouting match on Facebook over the Chick-fil-A restaurant chain. They didn't speak to each other for almost a year. Social media somehow goaded close-knit blood relatives to break fellowship over chicken sandwiches and an imagined link to the gay marriage issue.

We can easily come to believe that everything is in crisis, that the world is wholly dark and decaying, losing our joy in the ordinary things in life—little league ball games, our kids' dance recitals, an encouraging word for a struggling friend, sitting on the front porch with a cup of coffee and just being alone with God, or contemplating all we have to be thankful for, especially the depth of God's mercy and the wonders of His grace.

That grace truly is amazing. Any time I look back at my life—the good and bad, the successes and failures, my shortcomings and flaws, where I came from, and what I've been through—I am filled with awe at God's goodness. I could have easily been a statistic, but God's amazing grace has always been there to save, deliver, repair, rescue, restore, and sustain. The good news is that grace is freely available to all.

I can't write about the importance of keeping the lamp of good humor lit in dark times without mentioning the legendary college basketball coach Jim Valvano—"Jimmy V," as he was known—who died of cancer in 1993. Eight weeks before his passing, accepting ESPN's inaugural Arthur Ashe Courage and Humanitarian Award with one of the most inspiring speeches in the history of sports, Valvano offered this invaluable parting advice:

> To me, there are three things we all should do every day. We should do this every day of our lives. Number one is laugh. You should laugh every day. Number two is think. You should spend some time in thought. And number three is, you should have your emotions moved to tears—could be happiness or joy.
>
> I just got one last thing, I urge all of you, all of you, to enjoy your life, the precious moments you have. To spend each day with some laughter and some thought, to get your emotions going. To be enthusiastic every day and, as Ralph Waldo Emerson said, "Nothing great could be accomplished without enthusiasm"—to keep your dreams alive in spite of problems whatever you have. The ability to be able to work hard for your dreams—to [see them] come true, and to become a reality.[27]

That's sound advice. Indeed, that's biblical advice. Charles Schulz once called humor "the ultimate proof of faith."[28] It's true. To laugh when everything is going wrong requires a confidence in something bigger than yourself or your circumstances. The person of faith can laugh when everything is seemingly going wrong because he personally knows a God Who has promised to "work all things together for good." He has the Apostle Paul's assurance that "He who began a good work in you will perform it until the day of Christ Jesus."

The book of Proverbs closes with a classic description of a woman of faith: "She smiles at the future." The fact is, *every* believer can do that. And we can also laugh at the present.

. . .

There they are—five key attributes that helped me not only *survive* the toughest test of my life thus far, but to actually *thrive* going forward. And thrive I did.

At the height of the Corporation Commission investigation affair, I'm sure there were many who assumed my political career was over before it got started. I suspect I would have been tempted to agree with them at a few low points along the way. Surely my name had suffered too much damage, even if that damage was unjust. Surely there was too much doubt about my integrity planted in the minds of too many people.

Yet they were wrong.

As I heard my mother say on many occasions, "God takes care of fools and babies." So it may have looked foolish to many when, in 1994, I launched a run for the United States Congress. Some thought "foolish" was putting it mildly. For one thing, the whole Corporation Commission mess was still fairly fresh in everyone's memory. What's more, my district had sent a Republican to Washington only one time since statehood—for a single two-year term back in 1921!

After winning a very close runoff in the Republican primary, I faced an experienced and popular Democrat challenger. All of the early polling showed it would be close. But come November we won with 52 percent of the vote. I became the first black Republican U.S. representative from south of the Mason-Dixon Line since Reconstruction. I joined Representative Gary Franks of Connecticut as one of only two black Republicans in the House.

My opponent in the election tried to use the Corporation Commission controversy against me, even though it was clear by then that I had done nothing wrong and had never been a focus of the federal investigation. Although that tactic obviously failed, subsequent political opponents tried it too, and that mess would follow me throughout the rest of my political career, even when I ran for a leadership post in the U.S. House. Congressman Steve Horn of California, the chairman of the House Oversight Committee, conducted his own investigation when those old charges came up and told my colleagues, "If you vote against J. C. that's fine, but if you vote against him because of the Corporation Commission nonsense, you're wrong. He did nothing wrong." I don't know if Steve voted for me, but I was grateful for his clarification. The more desperately my political opponents tried to hang that phony albatross around my neck, the wider my margins of victory grew.

No, the chairman of the Corporation Commission didn't do me any favors when he secretly used my name in trying to entrap would-be influence buyers. Nor did he help me when he threw me and everyone else at the Commission under the bus with his "can't give anyone a clean bill of health" statement to the press. None of it held me back, though. I came through stronger and better equipped for the challenges ahead. It all came about because God is faithful and because I learned to dig deep.

As you're about to see, that didn't make the next critical step on my journey of growth any easier. The hardest season of my life was followed by one of the hardest steps of obedience to God I've ever had to take. Yet it was also the most rewarding.

CHAPTER 2

DIGGING DEEP TO LET GO

*I will not permit any man to narrow and
degrade my soul by making me hate him.*

—Booker T. Washington

When I won the race to represent Oklahoma's
fourth congressional district in Washington, I
assumed I was finally leaving the surreal aggra-
vation of the Corporation Commission mess behind me.
The controversy had dogged me throughout my campaign,
but as it became clear that I had nothing to do with the
scandal, I pulled ahead in the race and found that I was a
"rising star" in my party, certified as such by the *Washington Post*:

> In a campaign season rich with drama, Watts has
> become for his party a dramatic symbol of color-
> blind politics—a black Republican favored to win

in a heavily white, conservative Democrat congressional district in southwest Oklahoma. Should he win the House seat being vacated by Democrat Dave McCurdy—and polls show him ahead—Watts would "rapidly emerge as a leader in that class [of 1994] and have an impact across the entire country," said [Newt Gingrich], the House Republican whip who campaigned for Watts last week.[1]

In January 1995, I joined the freshman class of the 104th Congress, my party holding a majority in the House of Representatives for the first time in more than forty years. As I looked for an affordable place to live in the Washington area (no small feat) and set up my office in the Longworth House Office Building, I began to think that the scandal that had somehow ensnared me back in Oklahoma was ancient history. I was wrong.

VENDETTA

After I was elected to Congress, it wasn't unusual for Republican office-seekers in Oklahoma and around the country to ask for my endorsement. A team player eager to see Republicans elected, I was happy to oblige. But then something strange happened. Some of the people I'd endorsed told me they had received a packet of information from a Republican office-holder in Oklahoma—a member of the Corporation Commission—directing their attention to the innuendo and speculation from the height of the media frenzy over the now-closed FBI investigation. The packets were obviously intended to cause the recipients to rethink their request for my endorsement. The effort failed uniformly, my endorsement was still welcomed by all who received it. Yet it was clear to me that my former colleague back home—the fellow Republican who was responsible for so much vexation during my tenure on the Corporation Commission—was carrying out some sort of vendetta.

This gentleman began to occupy way too large a place in my thoughts. I couldn't imagine what was motivating his vindictive behavior, turning the question over and over in my mind, considering every imaginable grievance. Had I done something to him? To my knowledge I'd never done anything but wish him well.

Was it my race? I didn't want to think so. I've always been slow to attribute any person's unpleasant behavior to racism. When you get bad service at the restaurant, it's almost always because the server is having a bad day or is simply bad at his job. I knew better than to assume that every slight or injury was the product of racial animus.

Was it professional jealousy or spite? That seemed to be the most plausible explanation, but I simply didn't know. He had lost his own race for Congress (in a different district) in 1992, getting only 32 percent of the vote. Perhaps my success, which put me in the spotlight so soon after his disappointment, aggravated some bad feelings. All I knew was that his shadowy smear campaign was hurtful and wrong. I had already struggled with resentment and anger toward this man, and now I felt my heart going down a path that no Christian's heart should travel. It alarmed me.

I have always believed and taught young people that the way we respond to hurt or offense is important. Hate is a deadly poison to the human soul. I also believe that no one arrives at genuine hatred overnight. There is a progression that leads to a dark, destructive place. Hurt becomes anger. Anger, nursed and fed over time, becomes bitterness. Bitterness, unless uprooted, turns into hate. And hate, fully formed and deeply rooted, is antithetical to a God Who *is* love.

No Christian can hate another one of God's amazing human creations and stay right with Him. I knew this. I taught this. I believed this. Yet I could feel myself moving step by step down into that darkness. I knew if I didn't do something, I was going to end up hating this person with a hate that would destroy me.

WRESTLING WITH GOD AND MYSELF

You know you have a problem in your heart when just the mention of a person's name provokes a physical reaction. The hurt and anger I was feeling toward this man had begun to manifest itself that way in me. I'd hear his name and would feel an instantaneous knot in my stomach, and the best of moods would turn sour. A perfectly good day could be ruined in a moment.

God began gently but consistently dealing with me about the way I was feeling. To my shock and dismay, He was speaking to me about apologizing to my former colleague for harboring bitterness in my heart toward him. *Me? Apologize to him?* I didn't want to hear it. So I brushed aside those pokes and prompts with rationalizations, the same excuses we all resort to when we don't want to forgive someone and release an offense suffered:

I have not wronged this man. He's wronged me.

Lord, why should I apologize? I'm the victim here.

The man hasn't even owned up to what he did, much less asked for my forgiveness.

If I forgive him, I'll be condoning what He did—sending a message that it wasn't wrong.

These rationalizations become comfort food for us. We want to eat it over and over.

None of these arguments seemed particularly persuasive or impressive to God. He kept after me. My fallback strategy was to search the Scriptures for a verse I could use to justify my stance, flipping back and forth through my well-worn, marked-up Bible in a desperate search for a loophole.

I failed. Instead I kept coming across passages such as Ephesians 4:31–32: "Get rid of all bitterness, rage, anger, harsh words, and slander, as well as all types of evil behavior. Instead, be kind to each other, tenderhearted, forgiving one another, just as God through Christ has forgiven you."[2] Or Christ's words in the eleventh chapter of Mark's gospel: "And whenever you stand praying, if you have anything against anyone, forgive him, that your Father in heaven may also forgive you your trespasses. But if you do not forgive, neither will your Father in heaven forgive your trespasses."[3]

In one session of loophole-searching, I came across Matthew 18:21–22: "Then Peter came to Him and said, 'Lord, how often shall my brother sin against me, and I forgive him? Up to seven times?' Jesus said to him, 'I do not say to you, up to seven times, but up to seventy times seven.'"[4] Then I came to the parable of the unforgiving servant, whose master had forgiven him an enormous debt but who in turn showed no mercy on a fellow servant who owed him a small amount. Jesus ends the parable by warning, "In anger his lord delivered him to the jailers, till he should pay all his debt. So also my heavenly Father will do to every one of you, if you do not forgive your brother from your heart."[5] I have been forgiven much by a merciful God. I was profoundly aware of that, but it was going to be extraordinarily hard to walk out what the God-breathed words on those pages were telling me to do.

As Pastor Chuck Swindoll once said, "Forgiveness is not an elective in the curriculum of servanthood. It is a required course, and the exams are always tough to pass."[6] This exam was proving to be one of the toughest of my life, but then Providence intervened. One day in 1995, I received an unexpected invitation to an event in Oklahoma City honoring Cody Graves on his retirement from the Corporation Commission. Having joined the commission shortly after I did, Cody too had been subjected to unjust suspicion because of our colleague's perplexing refusal to give us a "clean bill of health."

Eager to see Cody and other friends and colleagues from the Corporation Commission, I wanted to go to the celebration. In the meantime, I started sensing that I should apologize to my other colleague for how I'd felt toward him, assuring him I would harbor no ill will toward him from now on. I wish I could tell you that I immediately submitted my will to the wisdom of God's Word and the promptings of His voice, but the truth is I resisted, explaining again to God that I was the victim. I was soon in a wrestling match with myself and with God.

It wasn't a flash of light and clap of thunder that ended my wrestling but the prompting of a still, small voice in my heart—the loving, patient, fatherly voice of God saying, "J. C., I'm trying to teach you how to do life better." That may seem like odd phrasing for a heavenly pronouncement, but those specific words rang with meaning for me. God knew this had been a simple prayer of mine for a long time. On more occasions than I could count, the cry of my heart had been, "Dear Lord, just show me how to do life better." I knew that if I was going to meet the challenges of being a husband, a father, a mentor, and a leader, I desperately needed God's wisdom. If I relied on my own strength and insight to navigate the turbulent waters of life, I would shipwreck my family and myself. I'd watched it happen to too many others. I simply wasn't willing to stumble proudly and blindly through my days on this earth trying to figure it out on my own. I'm too dysfunctional and too selfish. There was too much at stake. I really did want God to show me how to "do life better." That's the essence of this book, really. Doing life better.

So a few weeks later I arrived at the Jim Thorpe Building in Oklahoma City, resolved to follow through on what God had clearly put in my heart. Those hallways held quite a few unpleasant memories for me, but that first experience of elected office had nevertheless left me with some wonderful friendships, and I was looking forward to seeing everyone and catching up. My first order of business, however, was to make things right with my former colleague, so I went directly to his office and asked for a quick private word. "I just wanted to tell you that when I left this place I carried with me some bad feelings in my heart toward you over everything that happened while I was here," I said. "As you know, I'm a Christian, and God has dealt with me about that attitude. Those kinds of feelings have no place in a Christian heart, so I'm asking you to forgive me."

I'm not sure what I expected as a response. I suppose I hoped he would say something that, at minimum, would give me a glimmer of insight into why he had always been so friendly to my face but so malicious behind my back, even after I had left for Washington. That hope was disappointed. "Oh, that's okay, J. C.," he said with a shrug. "We all get that way sometimes. Don't worry about it."

That was it. No light. No heat. It was as if I'd just apologized for accidentally bumping his coffee cup.

If I entertained any hopes that my gesture of humility might cause him to alter his odd and hurtful pattern of behavior, I didn't have to wait long to learn those hopes were unfounded. Three weeks later he would be at it again. Word came back to me that he had sent one of his "love letters" to the state attorney general.

It didn't matter. I didn't go to receive an apology. I went to give one. And my willingness to apologize had brought me to a whole new level in my relationship with God. I didn't go to bring about a change in his behavior. I went to disentangle my soul from something that had me bound up.

I'd gotten what I'd come for. I was free—and on a pathway to being freer.

THE BEST REVENGE

Yes, I can look at a calendar and point to the day my freedom journey began. On that day back in 1995, something heavy and unclean was lifted off my back. Offense and anger nearly kept me from fulfilling my destiny and realizing my full potential. If I hadn't dealt with it at the root through God's tenacious prompting and goading, it would have robbed me of much of the joy, peace, and happiness I've enjoyed over the past two decades.

An old proverb says that living well is the best revenge. When we've been hurt, our fallen human nature wants to get back at the person who hurt us. Our brokenness drives us to return hurt for hurt, insult for insult, wound for wound, and loss for loss. How much misery in the world today is the result of the human instinct to seek revenge! The spirit of retribution keeps blood and tears flowing all over planet Earth.

Just like self-pity and bitterness, seeking revenge does more damage to the seeker than the target. That's why it's said that if you're hell-bent on seeking revenge, you should dig two graves—one for your enemy and one for yourself. Is it any wonder Jesus offered His shocking advice to "turn the other cheek" to a culture steeped in centuries of "an eye for an eye"? No, the best "revenge" is to forgive and move on, thereby allowing God to bless you and shape you into the best possible version of *you*. I'm so thankful I let God teach me this fundamental key to doing life better.

I'm doubly grateful that God walked me through this often-painful experience, because it has equipped me to encourage a lot of other people facing similar struggles. In my travels across the country I've had the opportunity to talk to many other wounded or hurting people about how destructive it is to refuse to forgive. It's interesting how I now seem to encounter such people wherever I go. In each case, it's been my privilege to point the way out of that dark valley. The only reason I can do so is that I have been in that valley myself. Trust me, it's grim down there.

Some of these friends have suffered horrific abuse, often from the very people who should have been protecting them. Some have been subjected to more pain than I can imagine. I will tell you what I told them. Forgiving doesn't make the person who hurt you right, it makes you free. Releasing him from his debt to you actually releases you from an invisible prison. Giving up your desire to see that other person pay a price brings you a windfall of emotional and spiritual wealth. Abandoning your identity as "victim" ends an intravenous drip of emotional and spiritual toxins into your soul.

As I personally discovered, sometimes the other person doesn't even acknowledge that he did anything hurtful or wrong. But making your forgiveness contingent on an apology, an admission of guilt, or the other person's remorse places the other person in control of your soul.

OFFENSES REAL AND IMAGINED

In life, there are genuine, damaging hurts that we suffer. At another level, there are the things that don't truly damage us but do offend us. This feeling of offense is real. Then there is another class of offense: the low-level slights, petty piques, tiny tweaks, and perceived disrespect that are part of everyday life.

It is this last class of offense that seems to have our nation drowning in a sea of outrage. I once saw a humorous sign behind the counter in a little mom-and-pop store that read, "The world is a magical place, full of people waiting to be offended by something." Thomas Sowell, Ph.D., a revered elder among America's growing ranks of conservative black intellectuals, has observed, "Some people are in the business of being offended, just as Campbell's is in the business of making soup."[7] Professor William Voegli has written powerfully and persuasively about America's "Grievance Industrial Complex."[8] Somewhere along the line we lost our sense of humor. Today any off-the-cuff aside offered as a joke can trigger an avalanche of indignation.

When I was in the Republican leadership in Congress, I introduced a new chaplain, a Roman Catholic, to my colleagues as Father Coughlin. After his remarks, I told him that while in most neighborhoods they call you "Father," in my neighborhood we would just call you "Brother." The conference got a big laugh, and the new chaplain thought it was funny, but afterward I realized I had run the risk of offending several demographics. Fortunately, there were no reporters in the room to fan the flames of indignation.

In 2015, the comedian Jerry Seinfeld caused a minor media stir when he mentioned that he knows a lot of fellow comics who no longer take their stand-up acts to college campuses, where the tyranny of political correctness makes it impossible to tell a joke without offending someone's delicate sensibilities. Chris Rock, who is among those comedians, laments the power of social media, thanks to the ubiquity of smart phones, to whip up an outraged mob with terrifying speed. "It's scary," he says, "because the thing about comedians is that they're the only ones who practice in front of a crowd. If you think you don't have room to make mistakes, it's going to lead to safer, gooier stand-up."[9]

Comedians, at least, can prepare their lines in advance. Politicians, on the other hand, have to answer questions from hostile reporters and think on their feet during debates and town hall meetings. There is huge potential for "putting your foot in it" with an innocent quip or an awkward phrase and plenty of enemies ready to shine a spotlight on a poor choice of words.

Sadly, it's not just comedians and candidates who have to walk on eggshells nowadays. Hypersensitivity is everywhere, and victimhood has become a coveted status symbol.

Christians are by no means immune to this fever. Surveys and studies consistently show that a large percentage of people who quit going to church leave because someone or something offended them. For example, a study by Lifeway Research of "the formerly churched" reveals that 37 percent of those who stopped attending did so because of "disenchantment" with the pastor, a staffer, or a fellow member.[10] I suspect "disenchantment" is a prettier way of saying that someone hurt their feelings.

It's no coincidence that the rise of "identity politics" has paralleled that of prickliness and grim humorlessness. I've learned that when we human beings are under pressure, under attack, or wounded, we tend to retreat into our comfort zones, flying instinctively to what we perceive to be our core identity, viewing the attack or pressure through that lens.

For some, that comfortable core of identity is rooted in race, sex, or ethnicity. *I'm black. I'm Hispanic. I'm female. I'm Jewish. I'm Italian. I'm a Southerner.* For others it can be rooted in some other "identity"—being obese, disabled, single, or divorced, for example. Being a Roman Catholic or an Evangelical Christian can serve as a form of identity as well, as can membership in most other distinct religious groups. A whole field of academic study—Social Identity Theory—has emerged around this new tribalism, tracking our society's increasing fragmentation into smaller and smaller "microcultures."

An episode of *Seinfeld* illustrates the power of identity over the human mind. Jerry is at a diner with his "Uncle Leo," whose hamburger is served medium-well instead of medium, as he ordered it. Leo concludes, absurdly, that the cook is anti-Semitic, and Jerry is unable to convince him otherwise.

Don't misunderstand—I'm not suggesting that people don't do truly offensive and hateful things because of someone's race, sex, religion, or other identity. I know it happens with heartbreaking regularity, because I've been on the receiving end of my share of racist actions and words, some of them deeply humiliating and infuriating. On more than one occasion, I've been pulled over by local police simply because I was a black man driving or walking where someone thought I didn't belong. Shortly after I was sworn in as a U.S. congressman, I was pulled over in broad daylight in Norman, Oklahoma, not by one or two police officers but by six! I wasn't disrespectful or uncooperative, but I did insist on knowing why I'd been pulled over. One officer told me they had gotten a suspected DUI call on me. As a matter of fact, I don't drink, and they never tested me. I might have understood a traffic stop conducted by one or perhaps even two patrol cars. But *six* cars for one innocent driver in the middle of the day was extreme. I later received a private apology from the police chief—the operative word being *private*. The kind of humiliation to which I had been subjected tends to be public, but it seems the apologies rarely are.

During the Christmas shopping season of 2013, I was in a Norman department store that my family frequented and where many of the staff members were familiar with my wife and me. I was dressed casually in jeans, a Eufaula baseball jacket, and my favorite black leather cap. The store wasn't especially crowded, but there were quite a few other shoppers present.

Moving through the various sections of the men's department, I became aware of a man hovering at a distance, and I wondered, "Surely this guy isn't following me, is he?" As he continued his orbit, I decided to test my suspicions by moving to a completely different department of the store. He moved with me. I felt the anger rise up within me, but I didn't want to escalate the situation, and I certainly didn't want the local paper reporting that the former congressman was the instigator of an incident. I had no intention of making a scene, but I wasn't inclined to just let it go, either. So I approached the man and said quietly, with a bit of disbelief in my voice, "Sir, are you following me?"

He answered, not so quietly, "I'm doing my job."

"Is it your job to follow me?" I asked.

His response was combative, dismissive, and more than a little insulting. It also caught the attention of an employee and other nearby shoppers, so once again I was on display in an embarrassing situation. Mindful that I was a former elected official with a recognizable face in my home district, I was careful to remain calm. I approached him again and said, "Sir, I'm in this store often, people know my wife and me." He then said, "I don't care if you're the president."

Seeing I was getting nowhere, I went looking for the store manager. As it happened, she had left, but I did visit the department manager, who recognized me instantly, apologizing profusely when I told her what had happened. My wife and I headed out to the parking lot, but I couldn't bring myself to leave without helping that gentleman gain some perspective about how I'd felt during our encounter. So we turned around and headed back into the store looking for the officer. We found him talking to the department manager. She obviously had told him who I was, and he offered a robust apology.

I accepted his apology as graciously as I could, but I left him with a thought. I said "Sir, I accept your apology, but

I want you to know that I have kids and grandkids that come in this store, and I hope they never have to go through the humiliation you've put me through over the last twenty minutes."

Shortly after I had graduated from college, when the Beanie Baby craze was at its peak, my wife asked a store clerk about the price of a certain Beanie Baby. He told her it was $24.95. As she continued to shop, she overheard a white customer ask the price of the same Beanie Baby, and this time the clerk said it was $14.95. When my wife confronted the clerk about the discrepancy, he apologized, utterly embarrassed, and asked what he could do to make it up to her. Her answer was, "Just charge me the same price you charge your other customers."

Yes, I too have been followed by the over-zealous neighborhood watch guy as I've driven through neighborhoods house hunting. I too have been mistreated because of my race. So I get the anger. I understand the pent-up, cumulative resentment. The fact is, most people come by their identity paranoia honestly. I'm not saying that we shouldn't view clearly bigoted actions for what they are and condemn them accordingly. I'm only suggesting that it's vital to recognize this human tendency to view *everything* through the lens of our core identity when we've been wronged. That identity could very well be the motivation for the offense. Then again, it might have nothing to do with it. We must remain open to that possibility.

I am grieved to hear the word "racist" thrown around irresponsibly because indiscriminate use cheapens that word and robs it of its power. And using that terrible and terribly important accusation as a club with which to beat ideological opponents into silence poisons our civil discourse and tears at the fabric of our American culture.

LOOK IN THE RIGHT PLACE

There's a story that illustrates a principle that we should keep in mind when we're offended. A man walking at night in a city came upon another man down on all fours under a street lamp frantically looking for something. When the passerby asked what he was searching for, the man said that he had dropped a key and it was a matter of life and death that he find it. The other man offered to help and got down on his knees as well. After a lengthy search, the volunteer finally said, "Sir, we've looked everywhere for your key and we haven't found it. Are you sure this is where you lost it?" The other man replied, "Oh, no. I dropped it back in that alley, but the light is much better out here."

The lens of your "identity" can make it easy to look in the wrong place for the reasons behind someone's behavior. It can even be comforting to assume that the person who has treated you poorly has done so because of who you are. Yet where the human heart and mind are concerned, things are rarely that simple. People behave the way they do for a variety of reasons. We're all walking wounded. We are all dysfunctional. It's just a matter of degree. I always try to keep in mind the adage, "Be kind. For everyone you meet is fighting a great battle." How true this is! The worst abusers were usually abused themselves. The hardest people are usually the ones carrying around the most inner scars and wounds.

Outward appearances can be deceiving. When the prophet Samuel was searching for the future king of Israel, God directed him to the home of Jesse, there to discern which of his eight sons to anoint as king-in-waiting. Samuel thought he'd found the pick of the litter when God corrected him: "But the Lord said to Samuel, 'Do not look at his appearance or at his physical stature, because I have refused him. For the LORD does not see as man sees; for man looks at the outward appearance, but the LORD looks at the heart.'"[11]

There are two takeaways here. The first is that whenever we find ourselves in conflict with someone, the first place we should look is inward. I'm talking about following the example of the young man Samuel ended up anointing that day—the psalmist David—who went on to write, "Search me, O God, and know my heart; Try me and know my anxious thoughts; And see if there be any hurtful way in me."[12]

The second takeaway is that we need to look past the outward appearance, or "identity," of others. If the word "prejudice" means anything at all, it surely means thinking that you know something about a person's character or capabilities simply because you know his race.

We can't be looking under the streetlight when the alley is where we dropped our key. We have to look inward, because that is where the power is, particularly the power to choose.

The fact is, we can't control everything that happens to us in life. Circumstances, nature, and other people can and will inflict damage from time to time, and there is nothing we can do about it. In Jesus' parable about the wise man who built his house on rock and the foolish man who built his house on sand, storms battered both houses.[13] You can't control the storms of life, but you can control how you respond to what happens. Being offended is a choice. Remaining angry is a choice. Nursing resentment is a choice.

Somebody once asked Dolly Parton if she was offended by "dumb blonde" jokes. Her reply was, "Not at all. I know I'm not dumb," adding quickly, "I also know I'm not blonde."[14] It's a great example of how to choose not to be offended. I like what Chuck Swindoll said along these lines: "We cannot change our past.... [W]e cannot change the fact that people will act in a certain way. We cannot change the inevitable. The only thing we can do is play on the one string we have, and that is our attitude. I am convinced that life is 10% what happens to me and 90% of how I react to it. And so it is with you.... [W]e are in charge of our attitudes."[15] The only thing you can control is how you react when an opportunity to be offended comes your way. What you do with that opportunity will affect the rest of your life.

Sometimes we look in the wrong place by blaming others for our own mistakes. It's the easiest thing in the world to do. It's also a dead end road. Coach Lou Holtz once said, "The man who complains about the way the ball bounces is likely the one who dropped it."[16]

Jack Canfield, the originator of the bestselling, inspirational *Chicken Soup for the Soul* books, once warned, "You will never become successful as long as you continue to blame someone or something else for your lack of success. If you are going to be a winner, you have to acknowledge the truth—it is *you* who took the actions, thought the thoughts, created the feelings, and made the choices that got you to where you are now. It was you!"[17] I heard my dad say on more than one occasion, "In life, when you find yourself in a ditch, usually you dug it yourself."

Yes, some people face greater obstacles than others. A young black man from rural Oklahoma, I knew that as well as anyone. The climb might have been steeper for me than for others with more advantages, just as the climb might be steeper for others than for me. The fact remains that with determination, hard work, attitude management, and the grace of a loving God Who is for me, nothing is impossible for me. The same is true for you. There is no obstacle that you cannot overcome with God's help and a heart to do things His way.

Sometimes this requires not taking ourselves too seriously and choosing not to be offended by things that don't really matter. But if the hurt is real and deep, maybe you're not being thin-skinned. Maybe you're being attacked. If that's the case, it's not a matter of simply shrugging off a thoughtless slight, "lightening up," or trying to pretend it didn't happen. No, in those moments, doing things God's way is about offering heaven's most prized commodity—mercy. If we are to be engaged in the lives of others and make a difference, we have to show mercy and grace, because life can be hard and it can be messy. We're never more like our Heavenly Father than when we forgive a real and grievous wound.

"WE HAVE NO ROOM FOR HATE"

The storied history of Emanuel African Methodist Episcopal Church in Charleston, South Carolina, reaches back to 1816, nearly fifty years before the Emancipation Proclamation, a time in which it was against local laws for black Christians to constitute a majority in any church or to even learn to read. The original building was burned to the ground by white supremacists in 1822. In 1834 all black churches were outlawed for a time, and the body met in secret, much as the earliest Christians had done under Roman rule. With the end of the Civil War in 1865, the people of Emanuel began rebuilding, only to see the new structure leveled by an earthquake in 1886. The current building, stately and white, its classic steeple pointing heavenward, was built in 1891 on the *north* side of Calhoun Street, the south side of that street being off limits to Charleston's black citizens by unwritten but rigidly enforced law. When Booker T. Washington spoke there on a March night in 1909, twenty-five hundred people, including many of the city's most distinguished white citizens, filled the pews to hear the renowned educator, author, and advisor to presidents.

Nearly a century later, in June 2015, on a typically warm and humid evening, a dozen of Emanuel's most faithful gathered for prayer in their fellowship hall. Among them were eighty-seven-year-old Susie Jackson, seventy-four-year-old Daniel Simmons Sr., seventy-year-old Ethel Lance, Senior Pastor Clementa Pinckney, and eight others. The youngest was the eleven-year-old granddaughter of Felicia Sanders. The twelve were joined by a stranger—a gangly, awkward white man around the age of twenty-one. They welcomed him warmly and learned his name—a name everyone in America would soon know—Dylann Roof.

Together the group read a passage from the eleventh chapter of the Gospel of Mark, in which Jesus is teaching His disciples about prayer, faith, and forgiveness:

> Truly I say to you, whoever says to this mountain, "Be taken up and cast into the sea," and does not doubt in his heart, but believes that what he says is going to happen, it will be granted him. Therefore I say to you, all things for which you pray and ask, believe that you have received them, and they will be granted you. Whenever you stand praying, forgive, if you have anything against anyone, so that your Father who is in heaven will also forgive you your transgressions. But if you do not forgive, neither will your Father who is in heaven forgive your transgressions.[18]

A discussion of the passage followed, along with some testimony, some sharing of burdens, and giving of thanks for blessings received and prayers answered. Then the young visitor rose to speak. Everyone turned to him to listen. "I'm here to kill black people," he announced calmly. He then pulled out a handgun and began shooting.

Three of the twelve—including Felicia Sanders and her granddaughter—miraculously survived. Felicia has no memory of saving her granddaughter by pulling her under a table, but she vividly recalls her bleeding, twenty-six-year-old son crawling across the floor to reach his dying great aunt. He was stroking her hair, trying to comfort her, when he took his last breath.

The massacre, though not unprecedented, was profoundly shocking to the nation. Sadly, it seems like every few years some deeply troubled young man with a gun takes innocent lives in a killing spree that makes no sense to regular folks. Columbine, Virginia Tech, Sandy Hook, and Washington Navy Yard have become bywords for senseless sorrow. But as appalling as this slaughter of innocents was, what followed left the world in disbelief and wonder.

Two days after this mass murder inspired by blind racial hatred, Dylann Roof was in court, and the survivors of his victims were allowed to speak to the young man who had broken their hearts. And every one of them refused anger. With the bodies of their loved ones not yet in the ground, they didn't lash out or call for retribution. They refused to perpetuate the cycle of hate.

In the greatest tribute to the legacy of the Reverend Martin Luther King I've witnessed in my lifetime, these genuine Christians reflected the spirit of Christ. When Nadine Collier got the opportunity to speak to the man who shot and killed her seventy-year-old mother simply because she was black, she said, "You took something really precious from me. I will never talk to her again. But I forgive you, and have mercy on your soul. You hurt me. You hurt a lot of people. But God forgives you. I forgive you."[19]

Felicia Sanders said, "We welcomed you Wednesday night in our Bible study with open arms. You have killed some of the most beautiful people that I know. As we said in the Bible study, we enjoyed you, but may God have mercy on you."

"I forgive you, and my family forgives you," said Anthony Thompson, who lost his wife that night. Thompson went on to encourage the young man to give his life to Christ.

The grandson of the murdered Daniel Simmons said, "Although my grandfather and the other victims died at the hands of hate, this is proof—everyone's plea for your soul is proof—they lived in love. And their legacies will live in love, so hate won't win."

Another relative said, "I am very angry, [but] we are the family that love built. We have no room for hate, so I have to forgive."

What an extravagant, sweet-smelling sacrifice these believers laid upon the altar of God that day. Mercy isn't cheap. It costs dearly to extend it, but its alternative—bitterness and hatred—is even more exacting on the soul in the long run.

Jesus was quite clear on this point: if we think we'll ever be in need of mercy or forgiveness—and we all will—we must extend it to others. As St. Francis of Assisi said, "It is in pardoning that we are pardoned." Neither you nor I can afford to hold on to hurts or wrongs or injustices suffered.

We have to call on God's grace for letting go, trusting Him to work us through that process of forgiving.

I once told an elite athlete who was about to have knee surgery that the surgery isn't the tough part, it's the rehab that will test you. The same is true of mercy. Saying "I forgive you" is easy. It's the living it out that is hard.

CHAPTER 3

UNLEARN AND RETHINK

Progress is impossible without change, and those who cannot change their minds cannot change anything.

—George Bernard Shaw

They're some of the rarest things on earth. Only five of them have ever been found. If you were to come across one, it would fetch a price per ounce ten times greater than the going rate for gold. They're freshly fallen "Martian meteorites," chunks of the planet Mars that got blasted into space through some sort of collision and eventually landed on earth as fiery meteorites.

Even rarer than a Martian meteorite is the chemical element astatine. If you gathered up all the astatine on the earth, it would barely fill a teaspoon.

The rarest feat in professional team sports is probably the "three-peat," winning the league championship three years running. The last team to pull it off was the Los Angeles Lakers with its NBA championships in 2000, 2001, and 2002. There has never been a three-peat in the NFL. Because of salary caps and free agency, it may never happen in any major sport again.

But rarer than a Martian meteorite, astatine, or a major league three-peat is an adult who's willing to change his mind about something of importance. I'm talking about a person willing to look at new evidence or to consider a new vantage point rather than reflexively defending what he has always believed to be true.

It goes without saying that we should be principled, but we also must understand the difference between principle and arrogance. I have seen elected officials dig in on half-baked positions that fit the narrative they've adopted, refusing to consider a better idea when one emerges. That's not principle, that's arrogance. Blacks and whites, liberals and conservatives, atheists and people of faith—like belligerent panelists on a contentious cable news show—are all talking past one another, more intent on scoring points than on connecting, shouting to be heard but never listening, seeking validation and vindication rather than truth and light.

I have identified three causes of this narrow-mindedness. Let's look at them one by one, and then we'll see what we can do about it.

1. CONFIRMATION BIAS

I was sitting in the "green room" of a cable news network waiting to go on the air, joined by a couple of my fellow panelists. It was the final year of George W. Bush's presidency, his approval ratings in the tank, much of the nation suffering from a serious case of "Bush Fatigue," and I was the conservative Republican for this discussion. I was chatting with one of the other panelists, a friend and liberal journalist, when he suddenly blurted out, "I hate that man." "Who?" I replied. "George Bush. I just hate him." Before I could respond he moved on to another topic, leaving me startled by the intensity of his antipathy.

A few years later, well into the second term of Barack Obama's presidency, I found myself in an airport with the same gentleman, talking about the groundswell of opposition across the country to the president's radical initiative to overhaul the country's healthcare system. This time he said to me, "I don't understand why people hate Obama so much. He's our president. Why do they hate him so much? It's wrong." Stunned, I thought, "Aren't you the same guy who several years ago was telling me how much he hated the previous occupant of the White House?" This man wasn't a hypocrite. He was genuinely blind to the contradiction. He was a victim of confirmation bias.

Briefly mentioned in Chapter One, confirmation bias is "the tendency to search for, interpret, favor, and recall information in a way that confirms one's beliefs."[1] It's sometimes called "my-side bias" because it reassures us that our side of a question is right—even when we're wrong. Confirmation bias is a special lens for our eyes and a filter for our memory.

Let's say for example that you've developed a belief that young black men are dangerous and prone to criminal activity. Every time you encounter a news story or an anecdote that harmonizes with that belief, you'll "see" it and tend to remember it. Your belief has been validated—which feels good, by the way—and more deeply entrenched.

What about news stories and anecdotes about non-black young men committing crimes? Your special lenses will make you much less likely to notice, and therefore remember, this evidence. If you are forced to notice them, the confirmation bias wiring in your brain will help you dismiss them as anomalies, exceptions to the rule, and therefore not meaningful.

I don't mean to single out white folks here. Every human being is prone to this error. I see it among my black family and friends all the time. If a person holds a core belief that white people are by nature exploitative and want only to keep black people down, he will take special note of every incident that harmonizes with that belief. That same person will be basically blind to information that contradicts that view and will dismiss as an anomaly every incident that doesn't fit the preferred narrative.

In both of these examples, a person never questions his core beliefs. Why would he, when the world seems to keep validating his viewpoint? The first and most important key to combatting confirmation bias within your own brain is simply recognizing that it exists.

2. COCOONING

It's never been easier to keep ourselves in a cozy, comfortable, insulated little bubble in which everyone thinks as we do and our views are constantly validated.

When there were only four television channels and three weekly news magazines, when there was no talk radio, no Internet, no social media, when neighbors talked to one another, you were guaranteed to encounter viewpoints that differed from your own. Journalists took seriously their professional responsibility to report the news fairly and disinterestedly. Reporters believed it was their job to keep government accountable, regardless of which political party was in power.

Times have changed. When I was first elected to Congress, a government jobs effort in my district was threatened. We ended up saving it, but a newspaper publisher there told me to my face, "Although it wouldn't have been your fault, I was going to blame you." When I pointed out to the editor of a Washington magazine some inaccuracies in a story she had run about me, she replied, "We are an opinion magazine, and those were our opinions."

With the advent of cable television, four channels became thirty. Then eighty. Then two hundred, and the number is still climbing. We no longer watch current-affairs shows searching for the truth. We watch to confirm our "opinions." At the same time, magazine stands have exploded with niche and micro-niche publications catering to every imaginable interest, taste, and opinion. Talk radio resuscitated the dying AM radio band. Then came the Internet, giving everyone a seemingly infinite number of sources for news and information. The most recent development, social media, makes it possible to build a vast network of friends, followers, and connections who think exactly as we do, feeding us a constant diet of confirmation and validation.

In this new environment, the nation's journalism schools have stopped teaching that a news organization's primary role is "informing the public" and instead inculcate the view that they must shape public opinion. Now the young people moving into journalism as a profession tend to be interested in doing just that—shaping the minds and hearts of the citizenry. The not-so-pretty word for that, of course, is propaganda.

It might be counterintuitive, but the more information streams we have acquired, the less ideologically diverse our daily lives have become. Fine tuning our media consumption, we spin cocoons in which we almost never have to encounter a viewpoint that causes us to question our assumptions. If a foreign thought somehow penetrates our bubble, our like-minded hoard rises up to mock and condemn it. When we're done, we can congratulate each other for how smart and enlightened we are. Given the sputtering rage any contradictory viewpoint seems to provoke in many people these days, it seems that life in the cocoon has conditioned them to believe they should never have to encounter an opinion that doesn't align with their own. This is no way to expand our minds and hearts.

3. NEW THOUGHTS HURT

When we're young, our minds are pretty malleable. This is why it's so much easier for children to learn new languages than it is for adults. It may also be why a majority of people who embrace Christ as Lord and Savior do so before the age of eighteen. Somewhere around the ages of twenty-two to twenty-four, our ideas and our world views set and harden. From that point, we have to work and be intentional if we're going to learn anything new or embrace a new way of thinking. It's not impossible, just painful— literally. Medical imaging reveals the patterns in the brain of a person being asked to change a fundamental belief or opinion are identical to those in the brain of a person in extreme physical pain.[2]

The legendary Chicago newspaper columnist Sydney Harris once wrote, "The three hardest tasks in the world are neither physical feats nor intellectual achievements, but moral acts: to return love for hate, to include the excluded, and to say, 'I was wrong.'"[3] He also wrote: "Our dilemma is that we hate change and love it at the same time. What we want is for things to remain the same but get better."[4]

I'm sure you've heard the famous definition of insanity as "doing the same thing over and over and expecting different results." It's unclear who first said it, but it keeps getting repeated because it carries a key truth. For example, you cannot eat and drink whatever you want, never exercise, and expect to lose weight. When my wife told a woman that a particular method of dieting was an effective way to lose weight, she replied, "Don't you get hungry on that diet?" In the last twelve to fourteen years, I've had to unlearn a lot of my eating habits. I'm not where I want to be, but thank God I'm not where I used to be. I had to change my thinking about diet and exercise.

Whether as individuals, church communities, business enterprises, or a culture, it is indeed crazy to expect things to get better if our actions and processes never change. If you want "better," you have to have the capacity to learn, to change the way you think about certain things, and to press through the pain of replacing some of your long-held beliefs. In other words, you have to know how to *unlearn* and *rethink*.

OVERCOMING PRIDE AND PREJUDICE

Just as there are three major causes of closed minds, there are three virtues you can cultivate that will make you the rare person with the power to change things for the better, both in yourself and all around you. The first of these involves laying down the sin of pride.

1. HUMILITY

Pride was the original sin. According to the Bible, it was pride that led to Lucifer's downfall. His appeal, in turn, to Eve's pride led to the fall of mankind and all the trouble and sorrow that have followed ever since. Pride is the mortal enemy of personal growth. The hardest person in the world to teach is the man or woman who already knows it all.

The Pharisees and other religious leaders of Jesus' day grew to despise Him because, in their pride and arrogance, they couldn't imagine that they didn't have everything figured out. He was asking them to learn anew what God wanted from His people and what the Messiah came to do and be. They would have no part of it. How could they? They had positioned themselves in the eyes of the common people as the ones with all the answers. They had images to maintain. The only one among them with enough humility to want to hear what Jesus was saying was Nicodemus, and even he would seek the Son of God only under cover of darkness (see John 3). I am reminded of something C. S. Lewis wrote in *Mere Christianity*: "A proud man is always looking down on things and people; and, of course, as long as you are looking down, you cannot see something that is above you."[5]

In 2012, my wife announced that, as a Valentine's Day gift, she wanted us to attend a marriage enrichment conference led by Pastor Jimmy Evans, whose MarriageToday ministry attracts couples from all over the country. I must confess that at first I didn't see the need. That ministry, I thought, was for troubled marriages, not "good" marriages like mine. My pride was in full force. In other words, I was looking down, not up. I eventually consented to attend and found myself learning a great deal about how to be a better husband. I had to take some difficult medicine, but it was a rewarding, enjoyable experience that equipped me to "do life better" in my most important role.

I almost let pride keep me from experiencing that blessing. As the book of Proverbs emphatically reminds us, we need wisdom. It's the "principal thing" for doing life better.[6] And the greatest obstacle to wisdom is a spirit of pride. "When pride comes, then comes disgrace, but with humility comes wisdom" (Proverbs 11:2). "Pride only breeds quarrels, but wisdom is found in those who take advice" (13:10).

I've discovered that most prideful behavior is actually rooted in insecurity. The insecure don't dare admit they were wrong or don't know something. Their identities are far too fragile for that. Only people secure in who they are in God can freely and humbly reveal their flaws. Over the last twenty-five years, I've met a couple of men I thought exemplified true humility—the Reverend Billy Graham and President George H. W. Bush.

In the mid-1990s, I spoke at a Billy Graham crusade in Oklahoma City. The great evangelist had supported Martin Luther King in the era of Jim Crow, had preached Christ to millions all over the world, had rubbed shoulders with kings, queens, and presidents, and had inspired three or four generations of my family, but when I was invited backstage to meet the legendary preacher, I encountered a man who seemed truly embarrassed by the attention he was receiving. There was no pretension about him whatsoever, and his demeanor seemed to say, "I'm amazed that God would put faith in me to do what he's had me do over the years."

I met President Bush in 1992 at the Republican National Convention. A few weeks later, he made a campaign stop in Oklahoma, and I was invited to join him for the twenty-minute drive to his plane at Tinker Air Force Base. It was just the two of us in the back seat of the presidential limousine. I thought he had made a nice presentation and I told him so. I'll never forget the look of surprise on his face as he said, "You really think so? I'm not a very good speaker, and I'm thrilled you liked it." This clearly wasn't false humility. He genuinely appreciated the compliment.

Here was the leader of the free world—the man who had freed Kuwait from the grip of Saddam Hussein, a former vice president, director of the CIA, congressman, ambassador, and decorated World War II fighter pilot— admitting to *me* that he wasn't a good public speaker. I witnessed that humility on several other occasions, such as when he campaigned for me and when my family spent time with the Bush family at their house in Kennebunkport, Maine. Mr. Bush was so humble that if I hadn't known it already, I never would have guessed he had been president of the United States.

Billy Graham and George Bush had little to prove. As I've matured, I've come to recognize that much of the bravado, bragging, chest-thumping, and demand for "respect" that I hear among the younger generation is really rooted in insecurity and fear. When we're trying to understand and connect with people who disagree with us, a little humility goes a long way. After all, it's one thing to believe, as I do, in absolute truth, but it's something else to start thinking you know all there is to know about it. In short, blessed are the humbly secure, for they have little to prove and they love to learn.

2. EMPATHY

People often confuse empathy with sympathy. We sympathize when we simply feel bad for another person, but empathy requires something more substantial. We empathize when we use our God-given imaginations to put ourselves in another person's shoes, to feel what he feels, to experience what he has experienced. Sympathy is relatively cheap. Empathy costs us something.

People nowadays are so unwilling to change their minds in part because so many of us have lost the capacity to empathize with someone who doesn't look or think or speak as we do. One business psychologist has dubbed this condition "empathy deficit disorder."[7] It's a source of personal conflict, of communication breakdown in intimate relationships, and of adversarial attitudes—even hatred—toward people with different beliefs, traditions, or ways of life.[8]

In its most extreme form, the inability to feel empathy produces mass murderers. Could Dylann Roof have coolly announced, "I'm here to kill black people," and then executed a roomful of kindly grandmothers if his capacity for human empathy wasn't broken? Could Adam Lanza gun down twenty first-graders at Sandy Hook Elementary if he had any capacity to imagine what other people would feel as a result of his actions?

We see a less extreme but nevertheless damaging level of empathy deficit in our policy debates. Refusing to put ourselves in others' shoes makes it easier to demonize or even dehumanize "the enemy." The language of dehumanization in politics isn't new, of course, but it has never been as safe and easy to employ as it is now, thanks to the Internet. Discussing an issue with someone in the checkout line at Walmart, most of us are likely to maintain a tone of civility lest we find ourselves beaned on the head by a can of creamed corn. But let someone hide behind a computer screen and give him the anonymity of a handle like AnarkyRyot666 and suddenly civility and human decency are gone.

The Internet is a mean, graceless place. Bishop T. D. Jakes has written:

> We've entered a new phase in the information age. What used to pass for news has taken a giant leap to public opinion and group-think supported by polls and consumer surveys.... In the shift, we have become so accustomed to the point-counterpoint argumentative style of communicating that we are desensitized to our need to actually listen to one another.... We can hold strong convictions without being acrimonious toward one another.[9]

The frightening fact is that careers can be and have been destroyed in a day by a social media lynch mob aroused to fury by someone with an agenda and a Twitter account. This is the way of the empathy deficient.

Empathy requires a genuine effort to understand not only another person's viewpoint but also how he got there, assuming his good faith, because most people do come by their views honestly. He may be starting from false premises or flawed facts. He may even be deceived spiritually, but he thinks what he thinks for a reason. At the end of the day, you might still strongly disagree, but you'll have offered the respect every person deserves and given yourself the opportunity to learn something.

Too many of us assume that everyone on "the other side" is evil or just plain stupid. Browse the comments section of any news-oriented Internet site, or even many Twitter feeds and Facebook timelines, and you'll see what I mean. People who hold different views are vermin, wingnuts, Repub-tards, Lib-tards, scum, animals, Teabaggers, knuckle-draggers—on and on the river of bile flows. Our opponents aren't simply misinformed, they're evil and clearly operating from sinister motives. They aren't simply mistaken, they're "liars"—correction: they're "filthy, no-good lying liars."

It's possible for two smart, educated, and decent people to land on different sides of an issue simply because they have different assumptions about what is true. I'm not siding with the postmodern folks who contend that everyone is entitled to his own version of the truth. I'm simply saying that name-calling and insults are a mighty poor substitute for reasoned dialogue and debate.

You may recall that the fifth of Stephen Covey's famous seven habits of highly effective people is "Seek first to understand, then to be understood."[10] You can't learn anything if you're not willing to offer the benefit of the doubt to people who don't see things the same way you do. You can't influence or persuade someone with whom you have no relational equity. In Washington, the Left makes a living talking to the Left, and the Right makes a living talking to the Right. The church should never find itself making a living just talking to the churched. God said, "Come let us reason together."[11] If it's good enough for Him, why not for us?

3. INTELLECTUAL HONESTY

A Harvard physicist has defined it as a virtuous disposition to shun deception when you have an incentive to embrace deception.[12] It means fighting confirmation bias and being willing to "see" facts and evidence that don't necessarily fit your preferred narrative of the way the world works. Like humility, intellectual honesty requires a certain level of security in who you are as a person and who you are in God.

Universities by definition should be bastions of intellectual honesty. Sadly, if an idea doesn't line up with the prevailing orthodoxy, however, a university can be one of the least welcoming places in our country. The other place where truth should be most welcome is the church, but often we're far more interested in defending our traditions than in stoking the fire of God's presence that led to the establishment of those traditions. Don't get me wrong, I passionately believe God's Word is the ultimate standard of truth and a perfect representation of reality. Most committed Christians do. But we flawed, fallible human beings interpret the Scriptures in widely different ways, reading them through our own lenses, flocking together with those who share the interpretation that fits with our own cultural biases and comfort zones. As a result, our churches can be as closed off to truth as the most politically correct campus.

The Baptist churches in which I grew up and I served as youth pastor were very conservative in their style of worship. Over the last ten years, as God has seen me through some difficult circumstances, I've encountered truths about worshipping Him that I'd never seen before, truths that

forced me to lay aside some of my former worship traditions. In the nondenominational church I attend today,
you'll find a more expressive style than in the churches of
my youth, with their piano, organ, and choir. A band and
praise team lead a congregation that is moving, shaking,
and raising its hands. All of this took some getting used to.

One Sunday in church, considering all that God had
brought me through, I raised my hands in praise for the very
first time. I felt awkward, simply because that wasn't what
I was used to. It wasn't wrong. It just wasn't the way I was
raised to worship. Yet when you understand that church is
about worshipping God, you eventually grow comfortable
raising your hands in praise and expressing passionate gratitude. Today I raise my hands in praise and never give it a
second thought. I don't care what the people around me
might say or think. This is the kind of growth that can happen when you don't think you have the final answers for all
questions.

PERSONAL CHANGE

I've already mentioned Stephen Covey's perennial best-
seller *The Seven Habits of Highly Effective People*. Back in
the 1980s, that book introduced the term "paradigm shift,"
which instantly became part of our cultural vocabulary.
Covey's book opens with an explanation of the transformative power of thinking about an old problem in a new way.
It felt like a revolutionary concept to many at the time, but
this was far from a new revelation. The Apostle Paul had
the power of the paradigm shift in mind way back in the

first century when he wrote to his friends in Rome, "And do not be conformed to this world, but be transformed by the renewing of your mind...."[13]

Unlearning. Rethinking. Upgrading your thinking. As we just saw, the Bible calls it "renewing your mind" and declares it to be the key to personal transformation. I've seen that demonstrated in my own life many times, as well as in the lives of people close to me. It's not possible to bring about lasting, positive change in your life—to overcome obstacles and break out of generational patterns of defeat—without first upgrading your mind in the area you desire to change. This holds true for politics, diet, exercise, or going to another level in our faith.

Of course, some people simply don't want to change. Winston Churchill once defined a fanatic as a person "who can't change his mind and won't change the subject." Leo Tolstoy said, "Everybody thinks of changing humanity and nobody thinks of changing himself." Others dream about change but don't really believe it's possible. They lack hope. Or they excuse themselves by blaming the circumstances of their birth, their heritage, or their upbringing. When a person says, "That's just the way I am," he is actually saying "I don't want to change." That approach won't get you to your destiny. An old saying reminds us that following the path of least resistance is what makes the rivers run crooked.

Dr. Caroline Leaf, a cognitive neuroscientist and a committed Christian, has written, "Change in your thinking is essential to detox the brain. Consciously controlling your thought life means not letting thoughts rampage through your mind. It means learning to engage interactively with every single thought that you have, and to analyze it before you decide either to accept or reject it."[14] How do you go about doing that? By "looking" at your mental processes. That may sound like a strange, if not impossible, thing to do. After all, you can't crack open your skull like an egg and have a look at what is going on inside. It is possible, however, to look at your mental processes. In fact, it is not just possible, it is essential.

In other words, start thinking about what you're thinking about. I'm talking about conducting an audit of the kinds of thoughts you entertain and the way you use your God-given gift of imagination throughout your day. Make a conscious, deliberate decision to monitor what you're dwelling on as you go through daily life. What you're looking for is negative, toxic thoughts about yourself or others. Thoughts often trigger mental "movies," scenarios in which you play out the negative implications of those negative thoughts. The Bible calls this being "vain" in our "imaginations," and the human imagination is a powerful thing.

You're not alone in carrying out this audit. The Spirit of God wants to help you. Ask for that help. I've already quoted King David's prayer for help in this very area, but it bears repeating here:

> Search me, O God, and know my heart;
> Try me and know my anxious thoughts;
> And see if there be any hurtful way in me,
> And lead me in the everlasting way.[15]

Once you've put your finger on the thoughts and imaginings that need to be replaced, you are ready to start interrupting and reshaping those familiar old patterns. The Bible calls this process "taking thoughts captive."[16] In other words, arrest negative, destructive, unproductive thoughts when they trespass in your mind. Yes, those thoughts are going to come, but you don't have to dwell on them. As an old-school preacher from Tulsa once said, "You can't keep a bird from flying over your head, but you can keep it from building a nest in your hair."

Of course, you can't replace something with nothing. The key to arresting a toxic, negative thought is replacing it with something better, something in alignment with what God's Word says is true. Knowledge of the Bible is the greatest weapon in your arsenal for personal transformation.

As Dr. Tony Evans, the pastor of Oak Cliff Bible Fellowship in Dallas, has written, "Where you set your mind is so important because what you set your mind on will penetrate and dominate your thinking.... [W]hen you set your mind on the things of Christ, you can receive God's word and allow it to act as a two-edged sword in your life. Ask the Holy Spirit to reprogram your mind with the truth of His Word, and then start acting in light of that. Not only will your fears and doubts leave when you come to trust and stand on God's promises in His Word, but God will build strongholds of truth in your mind and then stand guard Himself.[17]

It's also important to monitor your self-talk. All of us have an inner dialogue with ourselves going on during our waking hours, and much of what we say to ourselves, studies show, is negative. Many of us don't need any outside help beating ourselves up for our mistakes and shortcomings, but the enemy of our souls will pile on anyway. The Bible calls the devil "the accuser of the brethren."

He'll also give you lots of assistance in throwing a pity party. When your inner conversation has you taking on the identity of "helpless victim"—a victim of other people or of circumstances—it's easy to talk yourself right into thinking the whole world is against you and that God is too.

Athletes have to cultivate the skill of mentally bouncing back from a mistake. In the heat of competition, beating yourself up and running yourself down after a bad decision is deadly. The longest journeys I ever had to make were from the visitors' side of the field to my team's bench after I'd fumbled the ball or thrown an interception. The entire journey, I was tempted to tell myself what a knuckleheaded decision I'd just made or how stupid I was to fumble the ball. To make matters worse, my opponent was usually gabbing at me as well, trying to remind me that I really was an idiot.

I eventually learned to master the process of dealing with bad plays. First, I would process precisely what went wrong on the play so I could improve on it the next time it was called. Then I would tell myself to "let the bad things go. Don't dwell on it." I also had pretty good defenses at Oklahoma, and that helped minimize the consequences of a turnover, but letting go of the bad thoughts was still critical.

I was never a tennis player or a golfer, but I watch those sports closely. The mental game is important in any competition, but especially in those sports. You're competing more with yourself than with your opponent, and there's no one else on the field to cover your mistakes.

The field of sports psychology is devoted to helping professional athletes and Olympians manage their mental processes and inner dialogue. Yet you don't need a three-hundred-dollar-an-hour consultant to help you turn your inner critic into an inner coach. You just need God's help, His Word, and a willingness to dig deep to improve your thinking. You have to *choose* to set aside limiting beliefs and patterns of perception that are contrary to the truth.

The subject of *choosing* brings me to another simple but often overlooked key to personal transformation: simply making better choices. For better or worse, the life you're living today is largely a reflection of all the choices you've made up to this point. The life you'll be living ten, fifteen, or twenty years from now is being shaped by the choices you're making right now. And you have control over your choices right up to the moment of choosing. Then your choices have control over you.

The old adage "Don't just stand there. Do something, even if it's wrong," is not good advice in most cases. Not every choice brings improvement. For example, many people make critical life choices out of emotion, foolishly giving the reins of their life to anger, resentment, and sadness. Emotional decisions aren't ordinarily wise decisions. Coloring your view of the facts and disabling your objectivity, emotions will lie to you.

You need firmer ground to stand on, a clearer lens through which to view your options, when making choices about your life. That's why knowledge of the Bible and its unfailing, unchanging principles is indispensable for personal growth. Biblical principles have been woven into the fabric of the universe by its Creator. They apply to everyone, even those who deny that a Creator exists, and we ignore them at our peril. As I once heard a silver-haired preacher say, "We don't break God's precepts. We break ourselves upon them."

Finally, personal transformation is not possible without patience. Change is a process, not an event. I know this oh so well. It's important to respect the process, but you have to keep your eye on the promise or goal. It will keep you moving forward through discouragement or setbacks.

God can show you exactly what you need to do to change your life, but you may not like the prescription. God loves us in spite of the way we are. He knows I am dysfunctional, but he wants to have a relationship with me and encourages me not to allow my dysfunction to become my norm.

It's one thing to bring about improvement and even radical transformation to yourself as an individual, but what about cases in which change needs to be broader; and must involve more people. Is similar change possible for a family? A small business? A church? A large corporation? An institution like a political party? I believe it is. When an entire community of people needs to unlearn and rethink, it calls for nothing less than a change in *culture*.

CULTURE CHANGE

I have heard business leaders over the years talk about their desire to transform the organizations they lead. There are CEOs who hold themselves out as "turn-around special-ists." I've watched many make the effort, some succeeding but many failing. To succeed, a business needs expertise, knowledge, and talent. Expertise can be acquired. Knowledge can be imparted. Talent can be recruited. Changing culture, though, is hard. The best strategy, write the authors of a 2012 article in the *Harvard Business Review*, can't save a company with a poor culture: "Too often a company's strategy, imposed from above, is at odds with the ingrained practices and attitudes of its culture. Executives may under-estimate how much a strategy's effectiveness depends on cultural alignment. Culture trumps strategy every time."[18] And what's true for businesses is true for families, churches, even entire societies. They're all reflections of their own internal cultures.

Just what is "culture?" It's a group's deeply ingrained values, attitudes, beliefs, and assumptions, invariably and unavoidably reflected in its customs, habits, processes, prac-tices, and decisions, which in turn determine its experience of life. In other words, culture is destiny.

God built this universe around a set of principles or laws, physical and spiritual. As any driver who has tried to take a sharp corner too fast can testify, we ignore the laws of physics at our peril. In a similar way, we can't afford to ignore God's spiritual laws. This is just as true for families, businesses, and whole societies as it is for individuals.

Many a new CEO has taken the helm of a troubled company with a mandate from the board to turn the ship around. The new leader recognizes that flawed processes and poor decision-making are behind the bad results, so he

mandates different processes and institutes different policies. Those changes, however, don't always stick. Culture
trumps strategy. *The Wall Street Journal Essential Guide
to Management* puts it this way: "As a manager, you may
have the power to change your organization's policies with
the stroke of a pen. And you may have the ability to hire,
fire, promote, and demote people with relatively little effort.
But changing an entrenched culture is the toughest task you
will face."[19]

Cultures are rooted in traditions, and traditions can
work for an organization or against it, for an individual or
against him, but they are always among the most stubborn,
tenacious things in the world.

The University of Oklahoma's football program is rich
in tradition. When I stepped onto the campus in Norman
for the first time, I was immediately immersed in the history
of the place, especially of the football program. Songs, ritu-
als, ceremonies, and signs imbued us with the winning
culture of the place as quickly and thoroughly as possible.
I remember Coach Switzer's recounting the team's success,
reminding us of the Big Eight and national championships
the Sooners had won in the past. "Oklahoma has the patent
on winning," he told us.

The first time I ever stood inside the OU locker room,
I noticed a yellowed, aging sign over the door leading to the
playing field. It read, "PLAY LIKE A CHAMPION TODAY." At
our first home game, when the time came to take the field,
I watched as the upperclassmen reached up and touched
that sign on their way out of the locker room. Of course,
all of us lowly freshmen followed their example. I eventually

learned that the great Bud Wilkinson had placed the sign there as soon as he arrived as head coach in 1947. Soon his players began touching the sign before running out onto the field, and a tradition was born.

Coach Wilkinson clearly knew a thing or two about building a winning culture. He is arguably the most successful college football coach of all time, having compiled a record of 145–29–4 in his sixteen years at OU. His Sooners won three national championships and fourteen conference titles. Between 1953 and 1957, his teams won forty-seven straight games, a record that still stands. Without a doubt, cultural traditions can work *for* an organization or community—as they did at Oklahoma, but they can just as easily hold it back. Tradition is often little more than frozen success.

Changing a culture means helping a whole group of people unlearn and rethink. The problem is, for all the reasons we examined in the previous section on individual change, we don't like unlearning traditions. "Because we've always done it this way" is the refrain of failing and floundering enterprises. It's the collective version of the individual's excuse "That's just the way I am." It's simply an excuse not to press through the discomfort of change.

The novelist Somerset Maugham wisely wrote that tradition is a guide and not a jailer.[20] Nevertheless, it often chains us to outdated methods and obsolete ways. Mark Twain observed that "the less there is to justify a traditional custom, the harder it is to get rid of it." Nowhere is this truth more evident than in our churches. In congregations and in entire denominations, traditions can be so entrenched that they actually become a sort of "false god." To be blunt, it's a form of idolatry. Jesus once told the Pharisees that their outdated traditions were essentially nullifying the Word of God.[21]

UNITY, DIVERSITY, AND THE CHURCH

In the first century, when the radical, history-altering movement founded by Jesus of Nazareth was in its infancy, local church congregations were remarkably diverse. In houses and rented assembly halls, rich and poor, male and female, learned and illiterate, Jew and Gentile, representatives of every ethnicity within the vast Roman Empire, dined and worshipped together. They also faced brutal persecution and died together.

This unity in diversity is precisely what we should expect from a faith built upon the revolutionary proposition that "*all* have sinned and fall short of the glory of God," that "there is neither Jew nor Greek, there is neither slave nor free man, there is neither male nor female; for you are all one in Christ Jesus."[22] The ground is level at the foot of the Cross.

Yet in the twenty-first century, here in the most "Christian" nation on earth, our churches are among the least diverse places you'll find. More than five decades after Dr. King called eleven o'clock on Sunday morning "the most segregated hour in this nation," our churches reflect none of the robust, barrier-shattering power that characterized the Christian faith's first communities.[23]

No external power is forcing us to keep our black churches uniformly black or our white, yellow, red, and brown churches uniformly white, yellow, red, and brown. Yet long after legally enforced segregation ended in this country, God's people have clearly chosen to self-segregate. Of course, ecclesial segregation is not wholly a product of racial animosity, fear, or resentment. Part of it is simple geography, most people preferring to worship close to where they live. Cultural preferences in music and preaching styles clearly play a role as well. But the fact remains that Christians of all races and backgrounds still prefer to sit next to someone in church who looks and thinks as they do.

But shouldn't we expect a more inclusive vision from church leaders? Isn't the church supposed to swim against the current of this lost and dying culture? In other words, shouldn't our churches give that hurting world a glimpse of heaven here on earth? Shouldn't churches run to people of all colors when they have made mistakes, instead of running from them? Unfortunately, most pastors or congregational leaders simply aren't that interested in their churches looking like the United Nations. I'm not saying they'll die and go to hell if they don't, but it is still disappointing given what Jesus called us to do. Thankfully, there are exceptions.

The remarkable church I worship at is roughly 65 percent black, 30 percent white, and 5 percent "other," and that's no accident. Our pastor, Bret Fuller, and the other leaders didn't wake up one Sunday morning and discover, to their surprise, that there were many faces in the pews that didn't look like theirs. They have a vision of a congregation that reflects the diversity of God's kingdom, and that vision guides them as they foster a culture of welcoming inclusivity. As Bret, says, "We preach a sermon before we ever say a word." Another example of this diversity of God's kingdom is First Baptist Church of Fort Lauderdale, Florida, where I preach about once a year. Pastor Larry Thompson and his team are intentional about their outreach, and I see about fifty different nationalities represented whenever I visit. They too preach a sermon before they ever say a word.

Recall my working definition of culture: a group's deeply ingrained shared values, attitudes, beliefs, and assumptions—which end up reflected in its customs, habits, processes, practices, and decisions. You can't create a culture by enacting a few new policies or making a token "diversity hire" or preaching a sermon on race now and then. If culture flows first and foremost from values, then a church's leaders must make it clear in their teaching and their example that reflecting the diversity of God's Kingdom and the multi-colored breadth of His redeeming love is a core value.

Yes, I know many of my fellow conservatives recoil at the term *diversity*, but I don't. I certainly understand the weariness at the way the dominant liberal culture tends to reduce *everything* to identity group head counts and quotas. I agree with them that the ideal society is a true meritocracy in which every individual, regardless of race, is guaranteed equality of opportunity, not necessarily equality of outcome. In other words, a society in which the one who works the hardest goes the farthest. I recognize the irony of filling a committee, in the name of "diversity," with representatives of every aggrieved identity group and ending up with twelve people who think exactly alike. Yet I still believe there is tremendous value in *genuine* diversity. The first place we should find it on display is in our churches. I've discovered that a diverse body is a stronger, more vital, more *interesting* body.

A courageous black minister championed this vision more than 130 years ago, when the idea of whites and blacks worshipping side by side would have struck most people as madness. Born a slave in 1855, Elias Camp Morris obtained his freedom through the Emancipation Proclamation and the blood-soaked sacrifices of Lincoln's Union troops. A fervent Lincoln Republican, he became a respected minister and politician, promoting economic and social advancement through business enterprise. Morris was an organizing force behind the National Baptist Convention of black churches and a founder of Arkansas Baptist College.

In the decades following the Civil War, even as Jim Crow segregation took root across the South and the terrible reign of the Ku Klux Klan expanded even to Northern cities, Morris saw what an American congregation could and should be. In Paul's famous Mars Hill oration to the intellectuals of Athens, he found a biblical mandate for a multiethnic church that displayed unity in diversity to a watching world: "From one man he made all the nations, that they should inhabit the whole earth..." (Acts 17:26, NIV). In 1885, surveying the churches segregated by both law and culture, Morris wrote:

> Class and race antipathy has carried so far in this great Christian country of ours, that it has almost

destroyed the feeling of that common brother-
hood, which should permeate the soul of every
Christian believer, and has shorn the Christian
Church of that power and influence which it
would otherwise have.... [T]he whole world is
today indebted to Paul for the prominence he gave
to this all-important doctrine at Mars Hill.[24]

Don't misunderstand me—I'm not beating up on
homogenous churches. It's just my hope that more Christians will discover the beauty and richness of a church that
looks like Heaven rather than simply like "me." For that to
happen, we're going to have to unlearn and rethink how we
worship God and how we extend a hand to our fellow man.
We have to understand that to reach someone you have to
connect with him in the context of his culture rather than
expecting him to understand yours.

Whenever I think about this truth, I recall Coach Barry
Switzer's efforts to persuade me to come to the University
of Oklahoma. I was heavily recruited by schools across the
country. A parade of coaches or their representatives passed
through our humble living room in those final months of
my senior year of high school. All of them had a polished
sales pitch. Some even offered inducements to my parents
that violated NCAA rules. My folks never considered them.
They were poor, but they played by the rules and never cut
corners.

Although it would ultimately be my decision, my father
was leaning toward OU's cross-state arch-rival, Oklahoma
State, when Coach Switzer came calling one spring evening.

A revered figure in Oklahoma, he was especially well regarded in Eufaula because of the Selmon brothers— Lucious, Lee Roy, and Dewey—a hometown trio who had risen to national prominence playing for Switzer's Sooners. So unlike most of the other recruiters, Coach Switzer got invited to dinner.

Mother didn't put anything special on the menu for our famous guest, just beans, pork chops, vegetable salad, and cornbread, but prepared as only my mother could—ham hock in the beans, slow-simmered for hours, cornbread baked in an ancient cast-iron skillet from a recipe I suspect was handed down from mother to daughter for generations. From our garden, she prepared a simple salad of cucumber, onions, and tomatoes with vinegar dressing. In other words, we sat down that night to classic Southern soul food! Well, you would have thought Coach Switzer had never had such a meal. He went on and on about how much he was enjoy-ing it and went in for seconds on everything. At the time, and for many years thereafter, I wondered occasionally if that was all just theatrics and salesmanship. If it was, I thought, he's certainly a great actor, because he sure looked sincere to me.

Thirty-five years later it was confirmed that it was no act. I came across an interview in which Coach Switzer shared stories about his many recruiting trips for the Soon-ers. Asked whose mom was the best cook, he answered, "J. C.'s was pretty good." More insight came when I read his autobiography, *Bootlegger's Boy*, published in 1990, in which he tells of his impoverished childhood in rural Arkan-sas, a background not so different from mine or that of the people I grew up with. My mother's dinner must have reminded him of home. Barry Switzer came by his legendary ability to connect with black athletes—and poor white ones—honestly. He understood our culture and was willing to engage us within the context of our culture before gradually and patiently helping us understand a new one.

This lesson—that we can't overcome our racial and other divisions until we understand one another's culture—applies in politics as well as in the church. My fellow Republicans can't figure out why more black folks don't vote for them when it seems clearly in their interest to do so. But they have precious little relationship with black communities at the grass roots level. They haven't done what Jesus did—come and walk a few miles in our shoes, without judgment or condescension. Break bread. Discover what it feels like to be one of us. See things through our eyes. Try to understand why the average white guy might see an arrogant police officer as a horse's rear, but the average black guy will see an arrogant police officer as a racist and a threat.

This lack of relationship is why Republicans are so easily stereotyped within black communities by their Democratic opponents. Many black Americans have never had a meaningful conversation with a Republican or a conservative. They are a concept, an abstraction to the black community. It's easy to believe a lie about an abstraction, but it's harder to be fooled about someone you know and like. Most black Americans have seen Republicans only from a thirty-thousand-foot vantage point. They have no three-hundred-foot familiarity.

Another mistake we Republicans and conservatives make is judging a culture we know little or nothing about. We apply our own standards of what's right or wrong or what's important in this world. There's a human tendency to view what you're good at as important and what you're not so good at as trivial. When you grade your own test, you always get a high mark.

One culture may struggle with God's standards concerning sexual purity, but the other may fall equally short of God's standards relating to money, greed, and compassion for the poor. Both are falling short. Both need grace. But they're not "bad Christians" simply because they struggle in some areas and excel in others.

As for me, my blackness doesn't inform my faith. My faith informs by blackness. Not everyone is there yet. To their huge and growing black congregations—live in the pews and millions more on television—pastors like T. D. Jakes, Tony Evans, Creflo Dollar, Fred Price, Bill Winston, Michael Freeman, and David Payne preach a conservative biblical theology, holding up the Bible's moral standards as immutable and absolute. They also proclaim the values of God's kingdom without apology. Yet on Election Day, 90 percent of the people in those churches, if they are not too disgruntled to vote, will reflexively cast their votes for Democrats.

This apparent contradiction baffles and vexes many white Christians, to whom the Democratic Party's positions on abortion, marriage, and other moral issues—not to mention its general hostility to people of faith—seem incompatible with God's will for human society. Yet for the black voters in the pews, it's the devil they know as opposed to the devil they don't know.

And they don't know Republicans. By neglecting or ignoring issues of justice, we send the message that we simply don't care about what many black Christians are deeply passionate about. There is great pain there. The wounds of the past run deep as they do with all of us, black or white. A simple, "Hey, get over it, that's all in the past now" isn't going to bridge the trust gap. Many Christian political organizations in Washington seem to believe that people in the black Christian culture should abandon their priorities and adopt the white Christian culture's priorities instead. I listen to a lot of Christian radio and watch a lot of Christian television. I often hear lamentations about same-sex marriage or abortion or pornography and little or nothing about poverty or injustice.

Is it possible that you raise a lot more money in donations by getting people worked up over gay marriage than by challenging them to consider the poor and oppressed? It's hard to raise money around forgiveness or mercy. You can't get people out of their recliners over the plight of the working poor.

I'm not talking about messianic government. I'm not suggesting that wasteful, corruption-prone bureaucracies should shoulder our Christian responsibilities. We mustn't let politicians define grace, compassion, or love for us. In so many respects the church has allowed the politicians to speak for us, but political policies can't convey genuine love or grace.

Watch the talking head shows on both sides of the political aisle. Politicians use people and love things. Christians, when they are truly reflecting the mandate and example given by Jesus, do the opposite. God commands us to love people and use things.

God likes people that Republicans and Democrats don't like. He compels us to engage and embrace people of all colors and backgrounds. If we are going to be engaged with fallen, broken people—which all of us are—then we're going to have to operate in grace.

Grace is so vital because life can be hard. Life can be messy. I've been there and so have you. You may know someone going through a messy situation right now. We're all flawed and dysfunctional and require a Redeemer. I'll remind us again: the ground is level at the foot of the Cross.

CHAPTER 4

HISTORY NEED NOT BE DESTINY

The greater the difficulty, the more glory in surmounting it. Skillful pilots gain their reputation from storms and tempests.

—Epicurus

I don't care to be seen crying in public. Yet there I was, in a crowded movie theater, tears running down my face. And I wasn't the only one. Many other faces—black and white, male and female—were streaked with tears. The Oscar-winning film *Selma* made real and vivid what we'd only read about in books or heard described in Sunday morning sermons, the old black-and-white photographs coming to life in that remarkable motion picture.

What struck me most profoundly was the realization that I was alive when the events depicted in the movie took place. This wasn't ancient history. While my playmates and I were playing dirt court basketball in sleepy little Eufaula, men and women of extraordinary courage were placing themselves in harm's way to put right some deeply entrenched wrongs in our society. I was seven years old on March 7, 1965, known as "Bloody Sunday." That night, the grainy images transmitted from Alabama to millions of American living rooms shocked a complacent nation.

I'm sure my parents saw them, too. Our rooftop antenna, pointing northward toward the network affiliates of Tulsa, would have pulled in newscasts showing peaceful marchers leaving Selma, dressed in their Sunday finest. Hymn-singing marchers arrived at the Edmund Pettus Bridge—the entry point to Dallas County—where a small army of state troopers, local police, and scores of other local men, armed and deputized, awaited them. The marchers were greeted with a volley of tear gas canisters, followed by mounted troopers swinging nightsticks.

The next fall I entered second grade, one of the first two black students to attend Eufaula's previously all-white elementary school. I don't recall there being much controversy around the move, but a lot goes on in the grown-up world that you don't notice when you're seven. I do recall my own encounters with racism and prejudice. I watched my first movies from the balcony of the theater in Eufaula because black people didn't sit on the main level. And an odd demographical feature of my home town was that everyone who looked like me lived on one side of the railroad tracks that ran through town and everyone who didn't lived on the other, though in a small town where everyone knows everyone else, generational prejudice and cultural bigotry have a way of losing some of their edge.

Even so, a number of incidents in my formative years let me know in unambiguous terms that not everyone would be cheering for me as I pursued my dreams. For example, I couldn't help hearing the murmuring and grumbling in Eufaula when I got moved from fullback to quarterback in the middle of the third game of my sophomore year in high school.

When I was in junior high, there had been some talk about my playing quarterback, but I wasn't really interested, preferring to play fullback on offense, just as my childhood hero Lucious Selmon had done. (Lucious changed positions when he left Eufaula High School for OU, where he was an All-American nose guard.) I was good enough to make the high school varsity squad as a freshman. The following year, we found ourselves floundering at the quarterback position, with one guy who could run but not throw and another who could throw but not run.

My junior high coach, a fine man named Robert Newton, told Coach Paul Bell that J. C. Watts could do both. Three games into the season, I found myself learning a position I'd never played, while the town of Eufaula came to grips with something it had never seen: a black quarterback. This was several years before quarterbacks like Doug Williams, Randall Cunningham, and Warren Moon broke through in the NFL, pioneering what is commonplace today, and we were still three years away from Thomas Lott's becoming the first black starting quarterback in the history of the University of Oklahoma. Little did I know that six years later, I would immediately follow him as the second.

I practiced a little that week at quarterback but started the game at my usual spot. Our tough, senior-dominated opponent was loaded with talent, and by the end of the first quarter we were down 22–0. Desperate to shake things up, Coach Bell moved me to quarterback. The change worked. I started running and throwing the ball, and by halftime we had cut the lead to only two points. I felt like I was home. For the rest of my playing career—high school, college, and professional—J. C. Watts Jr. was a quarterback.

As I've already suggested, my big promotion was not greeted with enthusiasm in all quarters of our little town. In fact, when it became clear that I was the new starting QB, a few guys quit the team. There was the expected criticism, grumbling, and racist joking, all from the usual suspects, but I was confident that Coach Bell and his assistants would never let race enter into their decision. For them it was purely a question of what gave our team the best chance to win—end of story. Along with my high school basketball coach, Perry Anderson, a full-blooded Creek Indian, Coach Bell was one of the most important influences in my life. Those men and my father were the gold standard for manhood as far as I was concerned.

A few years later I was a senior at the University of Oklahoma and in my second year as the starting quarterback. Our team had gotten off to a rough 2–2 start. That may not seem like a catastrophe to many people, but trust me, by Sooner standards it was a disaster, provoking panic, finger-pointing, and recriminations. Our fans had become so accustomed to overwhelming success that, for many, a .500 record was unthinkable and utterly unacceptable.

It's a longstanding fact of football that when a team wins, the quarterback gets more than his share of the praise, and when the team isn't doing well, the quarterback gets more than his share of the blame. I was prepared to accept that. What I wasn't prepared for was the critical letters filled with ugly racial insults. Occasionally, the criticism was valid. When you run a high-risk, high-reward offense like the wishbone, the quarterback will eventually give fans some reasons to be upset. Yet many of those letters were just plain mean and racist—and usually anonymous.

After I lashed out in front of the press on one occasion, Coach Switzer called me into his office and shared a bit of hard-won wisdom. He said, "J. C., in 99 percent of the conversations you'll have with people about football, you'll be the expert. So don't waste your precious time and breath arguing with people who know less than you do." Then he suggested that his secretary, Kay Day, open and screen my mail, just as she did his, giving me the good letters and discarding the ugly ones. He concluded our conversation with another piece of wisdom I've never forgotten: "Don't let folks shoot at you in the dark." I carried that advice with me throughout the rest of my football career and all the way to Washington. If someone didn't have the guts to put a return address on a letter, I didn't open it. That policy served me well as an elected official.

As for that senior season at OU with the rocky start, we went on to finish 10–2, won the Big Eight championship, and defeated a very good Bobby Bowden–coached Florida State team in the Orange Bowl. I was voted MVP. In an interview with the *Daily Oklahoman* after the bowl game, a reporter asked me a question that saddened but didn't entirely surprise me. "J. C., I get letters from fans that say, 'J. C. Watts is a good guy, but we just want a white quarterback for OU.' What do you say to that?"

I pondered my response carefully lest any anger or resentment leak into my answer. I reminded myself that most OU fans didn't feel that way. The vast majority of Sooner fans didn't care what the quarterback looked like as long as he helped the team win. Then I replied, "Look. In my two years as a starter here at OU my record is 21–3. Those three losses were to two good teams. We've won two Big Eight Conference championships and finished the regular season ranked number three in the nation both years. We've been invited to the Orange Bowl both years. We won last year's Orange Bowl and I was voted MVP. So I suppose my response to those people is that my skin color isn't my problem. It's theirs."

As long as the people who mattered were happy with me, it didn't matter what everyone else thought. And the list of "people who mattered" was pretty short—God, my wife, my parents, Barry Switzer, quarterback coach Galen Hall, and my teammates.

"SICK OF BLACKS AND SICK OF FOOTBALL PLAYERS"

I experienced more of the same when I decided to run for the Corporation Commission. When a prominent banker in Norman responded to my announcement by saying, "Folks are sick of blacks and sick of football players," I wasn't sure whether to be more offended as a black man or as a former football player. The context of his remark was a series of highly publicized scandals that occurred within a forty-five-day period in 1989, about a year before I announced my candidacy. Three OU players were implicated in a rape, a player was involved in a non-fatal shooting of another player, and the Sooners' starting quarterback made the cover of *Sports Illustrated*—handcuffed and wearing an orange jump-suit after being caught selling cocaine to an undercover officer. Need I tell you the ethnicity of these players? The avalanche of bad publicity led to Barry Switzer's resignation as head coach after sixteen amazingly successful years—an outcome I've always felt was regrettable after his years of helping young men improve themselves and make better choices.

In that banker's mind, I was guilty on both counts—I was a football player and I was black—and I have to admit that his comment stung. But I kept my composure and said nothing. Any response would have been counterproductive, and I didn't want to do anything to confirm his or anyone else's prejudices.

Speaking of prejudices, my Democratic opponent in my first run for Congress found a creative way to play on them. The husband of one of my classmates from Eufaula, he had a copy of our high school yearbook from 1976, my senior year. Now, if we're honest, we all looked, shall I say, *interesting* in the 1970s. True to the styles of the era, in my senior portrait I sported a beige polyester leisure suit, an open collar, a beaded necklace, and an Afro so big there were some doorways I couldn't get through. Many of us who were young then look back and wonder why our parents let us out of the house looking like that.

My opponent featured that twenty-year-old picture in a campaign television ad, obviously hoping to arouse the distrust of the reserved, traditionalist voters of Oklahoma's fourth district. You can imagine the headlines had our party affiliations been reversed: "GOP Candidate Plays on Racist Stereotypes." But many on the Left believe that you're not "authentically black" if you've embraced conservative or libertarian views, and the reaction was muted. Several local black pastors spoke out against the ugly tactic, and to his credit, state legislator Kevin Cox, a friend who disagreed with me on some issues, publicly criticized the ad, as did state GOP chairman Clinton Key. That was about it, though.

When I arrived in Washington, a prominent black conservative told me, "As a black Republican in this town, neither the civil rights community nor the conservative community will come to your defense. You'll be on your own." Sure enough, neither the national conservative organizations nor the national civil rights organizations paid attention to the campaign ad controversy, and throughout my congressional career it was clear that neither faction knew what to do with me.

That was fine with me, because I was determined to maintain my independence. I had become a Republican because it was the major party that most closely reflected my values and convictions, not because I was in lock step with the party or its leadership on every issue. I'm still not. I have always believed that they can't take your independence, but you can give it to them.

My time in Washington taught me some sobering but valuable lessons about the glaring differences between the ordinary working people I knew out in the heartland of America and the cynical operators I encountered inside the Beltway. Far too much of what is said and done on both sides of the aisle in Washington is about accumulating and holding on to power.

I've also been blessed with an ability to see more than one side of many issues. I've discovered that things are rarely quite as tidy and clear cut in life as some folks wish they were. For example, in the fall of 2014 I was grieved to see our nation rapidly divide into hardened camps over accusations of police misconduct and excessive force after incidents in Ferguson, Missouri, and New York City. There were knee-jerk reactions all around as most people seemed unwilling to consider those events from a point of view other than their own. The usual talking heads from all sides rushed to the television cameras for another round of point-scoring, ax-grinding, and hobbyhorse-riding.

Whenever I was asked what I thought about those incidents, my gut-honest answer was, "I don't think the police are always wrong, but I don't think they're always right either." As I've already shared, I know firsthand that law enforcement personnel, subject to all the vices and flaws that afflict the rest of fallen mankind, are fallible. At the same time, my father was a police officer, and I have a son-in-law who is a police officer, so I have a lot of empathy for the men and women in that immensely difficult job.

I learned in Washington the truth of Lord Acton's maxim that power tends to corrupt. Because we invest our law enforcement officials with enormous power, it is essential to counteract the perfectly human tendency to abuse that power with transparency and accountability. I can't forget that some of the most humiliating and unjust experiences of my life have been encounters with people wearing badges. If I had let those experiences define me, they might have poisoned my future. By the grace of God, I clung to some principles that kept that from happening, principles I hope to pass along to you.

Sharing these experiences, I'm not looking for sympathy or trying to stoke the fires of racial animosity. I don't believe in collective guilt, and I'm not interested in victimhood. No, my aim is to help you overcome obstacles. These were mine. You have yours. The injuries, opposition, and adversity in your past don't have to control your future. And yet for many people they seem to do just that. If you understand why this happens, you can dig deep and start building the future of your dreams.

ANCHORED TO THE PAST

If the colossal sales of Pastor Rick Warren's book *The Purpose Driven Life* are any indication, a lot of people are looking for a sense of meaning and direction. Offering his readers an extremely important insight, Warren writes, "We are products of our past, but we don't have to be prisoners of it. God's purpose is not limited by your past."[1]

This is absolutely true. Yet I meet people all the time who clearly have the potential to live great lives, achieve remarkable things, and build amazing futures for themselves and for their families, but for various reasons they are prisoners of the past, trying to run a race with an anchor chained to their leg. Here are some of the most common anchors—things that keep you tied to the past and hinder your future.

EXCUSE MAKING AND SELF-PITY

George Washington Carver once said, "Ninety-nine percent of failures come from people who have the habit of making excuses."[2] It's natural. It's understandable. It's oh so easy. When you've been treated unfairly, repeatedly dealt a bad hand because the deck is stacked against you, there is a powerful temptation to throw up your hands and quit trying. When the playing field is tilted against you, making every battle an uphill fight, the understandable reaction is to walk to the sidelines and say, "I'm not playing anymore." Yet it's a reaction you can and must resist.

When the world has been cold and cruel, our fallen human nature wants to wrap itself in the comforting blanket of victimhood. And once you wrap yourself in that blanket, it can be hard to take it off. Some people wear the mantel of victimhood for the rest of their lives, making it part of their very identity. Offering excuses for a life of mediocrity, even valid excuses based on real tragedies and injustices, is the path of least resistance. It's not hard to understand why so many people take that path, but as we'll see in a moment, there is another way.

DISCOURAGEMENT

There is an illuminating old parable that preachers have told for generations. It seems the devil once announced a going-out-of-business sale and planned to offer his favorite tools to whomever would pay his price. On the night of the sale, each insidious implement—Malice, Hatred, Envy, Jealousy, Greed, Sensuality, Deceit, and other destructive tools of his trade—was displayed on a table with a price tag. Set apart from the rest of the collection, on a table all its own, lay a simple wedge-shaped tool that was more heavily worn and weathered than the others. It also carried a much higher price tag. Someone asked the devil what it was. "That's Discouragement," he said.

"Why is it by far the most expensive of the bunch?"

"Because," replied Satan, "it is more useful to me than any of the others. When all of my other tools fail, I can pry open and get inside a person's soul with that one. Once I'm in there with Discouragement, he's finished. It is so worn because I use it with nearly everybody, as very few people yet realize this tool belongs to me."

Discouragement may be the most common and debilitating condition in the world. It's also highly contagious. Whether we are faced with a single devastating setback or a long series of little ones, it's easy to become discouraged, and unless we respond vigorously, discouragement can color our whole outlook on life. That's a killer.

At its root, discouragement is a crisis of faith. It represents a loss of confidence that hard work and persistence will ultimately be rewarded, that God will come through. Someone who stops believing, down deep, that diligence and perseverance will pay off will not keep going when the rewards don't come as quickly as he or she hoped. To press through adversity and disappointment, you've got to believe that certain laws govern the universe, even if you don't believe in a personal God. You've got to believe that the laws of success are as reliable as the laws of physics.

Deep discouragement, in other words, is a collapse of faith in the existence of truth, and the person who ceases to believe in truth easily falls into a pessimistic view of the world and the future. Norman Vincent Peale taught "the power of positive thinking." Well, negative thinking is powerful too. A negative person expects the worst and usually gets it.

IMPATIENCE

A heavy dose of impatience sprinkled liberally with youthful arrogance once came close to costing me all the opportunities that have come my way over the past forty years. In Eufaula, I'd been the proverbial big fish in a small pond. I had enjoyed a lot of success, a lot of attention, and a lot of accolades. After Coach Switzer's recruiting visit to my home, I felt I wanted to go to the University of Oklahoma, and I was confident I would be getting plenty of playing time as a freshman.

It turned out that nearly every player coming out of high school thought the same thing, and we were all in for a rude awakening. The first reality check came early, when the Sooners' depth chart was posted outside the locker room. I was one of seven quarterbacks on OU's roster. *Seven!* Even worse, I was listed as sixth string. The dark force of discouragement latched on to my soul. A starter in every sport since little league, always in the middle of the action, I was now a faceless number riding the bench, and as the season began, although I had worked my way up to the number three quarterback, my discouragement deepened. In my immaturity, I decided to quit. I packed my few belongings and headed back to Eufaula.

When I arrived home unexpectedly, a family friend, Gary Moores, called Lucious Selmon, now an assistant coach at OU, who in turn told Coach Switzer I had quit the program. I'd barely had time to get my shoes off before Coach Switzer had me on the phone at my parents' house. "Come back and let's discuss this face to face," he encouraged. "Then if you still want to leave, I'll sign a release form so you can play somewhere else if you want." What he said sounded reasonable, so I re-loaded my car and returned to Norman. But I was determined to leave. This was an exit interview as far as I was concerned. Given Barry Switzer's famous charm, however, if my intention truly was to leave, going back to talk to him was a tactical error.

When I sat down in his office, Switzer told me, "J. C., if you stay you'll play. You've got a future here." I wondered if he said the same thing to every discouraged freshman who tried to quit, but he went on: "We will redshirt you next year," meaning I wouldn't play that season but my eligibility would be extended by a year. Then Coach said, "After that, you'll back up Thomas Lott for a year, and then you'll start for two years. You'll have a great career at Oklahoma, J. C."

I believed him in part because you don't tell a frustrated freshman he won't see the field for another year and a half if you're trying to talk him into staying. That's just poor salesmanship. As I would learn, that's also classic Barry

Switzer. He is transparent and frank, whether his message is likely to make you glad, sad, or mad.

I bought in. I decided to stay, work hard, and earn my place on the team. Over the next few years, my career unfolded exactly as he'd said it would: a redshirt year, a year of backing up Thomas Lott, and then two successful years as the starting quarterback for the Sooners. What a difference that one decision made in my life. It blessed me with friendships that endure to this day. It opened doors for me to speak and minister all over the country. It paved the way for me to play professional football in Canada and quarterback a Grey Cup—Canada's Super Bowl—team in my rookie year.

What if I hadn't returned to Norman that night but instead had let my impatience and immaturity get the best of me? I never would have been elected to statewide office, served in Congress, or enjoyed countless other blessings and opportunities, including writing this book!

Leo Tolstoy wrote, "The two most powerful warriors are patience and time," and Aristotle said, "Patience is bitter, but its fruit is sweet." Many people reject the bitterness of waiting or paying their dues. When they do, they are often left with another weight that keeps them anchored to the past.

REGRET

Deion Sanders is the only athlete in history to hit a major league home run and score an NFL touchdown in the same week. He's the only man to play in both the Super Bowl and the World Series. Deion Sanders is obviously a gifted athlete, but gifts alone don't guarantee high achievement. In fact, many gifted people don't accomplish much of anything, as Deion insisted in an interview with the sportswriter Mike Lupica:

> The best athletes in the world end up at home on the corner. Oh you bet they do. I call them Idas. "If I'da done this, I'd be making three million today.... If I'da practiced a little harder, I'd be a superstar." They'll be standing on that corner till they die telling you all the things they woulda done. I see 'em all the time. Guys who were as fast as me when we were kids. But instead of working for their dreams they chose a life of street corners.[3]

We all come down with a case of the "woulda, shoulda, couldas" from time to time. It's natural to look back with a twinge of remorse on an opportunity squandered or to wonder about the proverbial "road not taken." John Greenleaf Whittier's little rhyme has been cited countless times: "For of all sad words of tongue or pen, / The saddest are these: 'It might have been!'"[4] This is a part of life. Yet some people allow regret to become either a paralyzing toxin or an anesthetizing drug. In either case, it keeps them tied to the past and hinders them from moving into a better future.

I learned a lesson after my wife and I moved from Oklahoma to Virginia. Our new home had a three-car garage, but two of the bays were filled with "stuff" we'd brought from Oklahoma. Over the next five or six years, piece by piece, we gradually got rid of those things until all three garage bays were empty. When we were finished, we laughed at the realization that we had gone to a lot of trouble and expense just to move junk we didn't need half-way across the country. We should have left it behind in Oklahoma.

We do the same thing with our regrets, the mental and emotional "junk" that we haul from one year to the next, sometimes passing them on to our children and grandchildren. We refuse to throw away junk we should have gotten rid of years ago.

We might regret the things we haven't done but wish we had or the things we have done but wish we hadn't—sins, in either case, against ourselves and God. If we have sinned against others, we feel another kind of pain (provided our consciences haven't become too hardened)—guilt.

Deep remorse for past mistakes can be a powerful chain to the past. So can excuse-making, victimhood, impatience, discouragement, and regret. If you're tied to your past, you keep dragging it with you into the present and future, but it doesn't have to be that way. Your history need not be your destiny. Here are a few keys to breaking loose and stepping into the brighter future God wants you to experience.

LET GOD REDEEM YOUR PAST

If you read the gospels with fresh eyes, you'll be struck by how many people Jesus encountered and embraced who had a "past." His entourage included a crooked tax collector, a man with a violent temper who swore profusely and was inclined to pull out a knife when agitated or threatened, a thief, a former prostitute, and an array of other "undesirables." In fact, this was one of the primary points of criticism against Him by the proper, legalistic religious folks of His day. Wherever He went, he seemed always to be in the company of the "wrong sort of people."

Jesus' critics failed to comprehend two things. First, we are *all* the wrong sort of people. "There is none righteous. No not one."[5] Second, people usually came away from an encounter with Jesus changed on the inside. Time after time, people with much to answer for—the woman caught in adultery, Zacchaeus the cheating tax collection agent, the Samaritan woman at the well with seven failed marriages in her history, rebels, outcasts, and untouchables—found new and brighter futures after allowing Jesus to do His miraculous work in their hearts.

If you'll let Him, God can and will redeem your past, breaking the chains that keep you tied to past mistakes. Of course, when we've wronged or injured someone, we should do everything within our power to make restitution, just as Zacchaeus did. When restitution is not possible, we can express sincere remorse to the damaged party. But as important as it is to make amends, the complete remedy for guilt can be found only at the foot of the Cross of Christ. We're all flawed and broken on the inside, in desperate need of mercy and cleansing for our sin-soiled consciences.

As I noted in Chapter Two, it is precisely because we are all in such dire need of forgiveness that we must be prepared to extend it to those who wrong us. Christ Himself taught us to pray, "Forgive us our trespasses as we forgive those who trespass against us." The heaviest baggage we carry is often linked to deep wounds inflicted on us by others. Allowing God to "redeem your past" means giving Him all those things that Satan, the enemy of your soul, would use to damage or destroy you, so He can make them a part of your story of triumph. As Joyce Meyer likes to say, "Let God turn your mess into your message."

She knows a little about that. Her inspiring testimony centers on her emotional healing and restoration after having suffered many years of horrifying sexual abuse by her father. In her autobiographical book *Beauty for Ashes*, she recounts her journey from brokenness, shame, and anger to wholeness through God's love and power.[6] Today her worldwide ministry touches millions, and God has used her willingness to share her story to help tens of thousands of other victims of abuse, both men and women, find the courage to bring their darkest pain into the healing light of His love. In other words, she let God turn her mess into her message.

In a world filled with fallen people to whom God has granted the powerful gift of free will, evil touches every life. The misfortune of someone close to me or someone far away has often left me wondering, "Why, Lord?" That's when I pray, "God, help me understand."

Sometimes greater understanding comes. When it doesn't, I've learned to remember that there is a much bigger picture than any of us can see. Then my prayer becomes, "Lord, I can't see your hand, but I trust your heart." What I've learned beyond any doubt is that God is for me, and if I submit to and cooperate with Him, if I strive to follow the principles He has made clear in His Word, my life will take an upward trajectory higher than anything I could ask or think. The same is true for you.

PERSISTENCE

The most common reason people stay chained to the past is also the primary reason most people live far below their potential. They do what I came very close to doing my freshman year at Oklahoma. They quit.

Thomas Edison famously said, "Many of life's failures are experienced by people who did not realize how close they were to success when they gave up."[7] Life presents us with a wide array of good excuses to surrender. We've examined several of them—discouragement, adversity, injustice, unfairness, tragedy, and the simple reality that achieving exceptional things always requires more time and effort than most people are willing to expend. If greatness were easy, more people would live great lives and accomplish great things. Most "overnight success" is actually the product of years of quiet, thankless preparation and diligence.

We want shortcuts. We want miracle cures and wonder drugs. We want a "hack" that gives us the desired results without all the sweat, pain, and time such an outcome actually requires. In athletics, business, the arts, ministry, and every other field of human activity, achieving greatness requires doing the right thing the right way over and over and over again. Persistence—which also goes by names like perseverance, patience, grit, and resolve—involves digging deep to call on reserves of mental toughness you may not know you possessed.

Yes, you will face unfairness and adversities that no one else has faced, but that just means you will have to run farther, jump higher, study longer, and dig up more determination in the face of your struggle. I like what the pastor John Maxwell says about the virtue of persistence:

> The trials and pressures of life—and how we face them—often define us. Confronted by adversity, many people give up while others rise up. How do those who succeed do it? They persevere. They find the benefit to them personally that comes from any trial. And they recognize that the best thing about adversity is coming out on the other side of it. There is a sweetness to overcoming your troubles and finding something good in the process, however small it may be. Giving up when adversity threatens can make a person bitter. Persevering through adversity makes one better.[8]

Speaking of sweetness, on a mild Monday night in 1987, the amazing Walter Payton was beginning the final season of his extraordinary football career, having long since broken Jim Brown's seemingly untouchable career rushing record. When Payton, known throughout the NFL as "Sweetness," tore off a long run, the television announcer Al Michaels noted that his career rushing yardage amounted to nine miles, to which color commentator Dan Dierdorf quickly added, "Yeah, and that's with somebody knocking

him down every 4.6 yards." That's pretty much the definition of persistence, isn't it? Not surprisingly, Walter Payton's
motto as a player and a man was "Never die easy."

I can identify with that "never quit" ethic. I was taught
that approach early in life and developed a powerful streak
of stubborn determination. For me, it didn't matter what
the odds were or what people thought. Opposition only
made me more determined, especially if succeeding gave me
an opportunity to shatter a stereotype.

We have to take a lesson from the importunate widow
in Jesus' parable, the persistent, tenacious woman who kept
pestering the "unjust judge" until he gave her what she
needed (Luke 18:1–8). She was relentless. We must be too.

EFFORT

In 2015, Serena Williams hoisted the Wimbledon championship trophy above her head for the sixth time, complet-
ing her second "Serena Slam"—the extraordinary feat of
holding all four of professional tennis's most coveted titles
at once. It was her twenty-first victory in a Grand Slam
tournament.

Watching her celebrate her victory, I couldn't help thinking about the rarity of the man or woman truly willing to
pay the price to be a champion. In any field of endeavor,
those who rise to the top are the ones willing to run the
extra mile, to get up twenty minutes earlier to work out
twenty minutes longer, to refine their jump shot for another
twenty minutes after everyone else has headed to the showers, to gut out one more agonizing rep in that extra set of

squats, to study one more hour for the exam while everyone else is headed to the club. I'm talking about those who find a way to say "no" to a thousand tempting diversions so they can say "yes" to their inner fire to achieve and excel at one thing. I don't care what your skin color is, if you're ever going to stand in the winner's circle there is a price to pay. There are rarely shortcuts.

I also felt a twinge of pain for the opponent Serena had just defeated in two hard-fought sets, knowing personally how hard it is to get to the big game and lose. Nevertheless, I shower the winner of any championship contest with praise because I know how hard it is to dig deeper than your opponent and win. I don't believe in luck. I believe in preparation. When preparation meets opportunity, good things happen.

The same is true in every area of life. There's a difference between equality of opportunity and equality of result. I believe we have to do all we can to make sure people of all colors and backgrounds get equal opportunities. Yet if I'm not willing to take advantage of an opportunity, well, it's not the opportunity's fault. It's my fault. It's tempting to blame "the system" because that's less painful than pointing a finger at oneself. American society isn't perfect—not by a long shot—but the principles of success that we're examining here will work for everyone. Unfortunately, we have created an entitlement culture in this country, a culture that encourages people to think they're entitled to the job, the position, the opportunity, the rewards they want, whether or not they have put in the work or invested the necessary time and sweat. It's like finishing seminary in May and looking for a senior pastor's job in August. We've tossed aside merit-based individualism and embraced collective tribalism.

Sports is the one field that has resisted the entitlement culture. In a professional team sport such as football, that entitlement mentality won't fly for a second with your coaches or your teammates. You can't stroll into the huddle and inform your teammates that you haven't done your conditioning, studied the playbook, or attended the team film-watching sessions but you believe you deserve to be on the field because you've had a rough couple of weeks. Try that and you're likely to find yourself physically assisted to the sidelines. Everyone is there to win. Everyone is responsible for his part. Each game is an opportunity. If you're not willing to do what's necessary to seize that opportunity, there's someone right behind you who is.

In athletic competition, the opposition will expose you if you have bad culture, bad habits, or are unprepared. In fact, professional sports may be the closest thing to a true meritocracy that you'll find in this world. There's simply too much money at stake these days for anyone to indulge petty bigotries. The person who gives the team the best chance to succeed gets the job.

For some reason, many people don't think those principles translate to the workplace or the marketplace, but they should. As a business owner, I'm willing to give anyone a fair shot, but I'm no more likely to hire, promote, or keep someone who doesn't want to work hard than a coach is likely to keep a slacker on the team, much less offer a starting role.

Many people entering the job market today are products of a culture that doesn't teach paying the price. Management can teach expertise and skills, but changing a faulty culture is very hard. As a manager, I'd prefer not to deal with people who are products of a culture of entitlement. On the other hand, if a person is prepared to grow, take correction, and cultivate good habits, I want him on my team no matter who he is.

I love coach Bobby Knight's famous comment, "The key is not the will to win: everybody has that. It is the will to *prepare* to win that is important."[9] For the record, Knight was actually paraphrasing Bud Wilkinson.

That's the kind of person I've tried to be, and it's what I'm looking for in team members. My attitude has always been just give me a chance. It doesn't even have to be a fair chance. Most of the time I'll succeed because I'll be the most determined to win. I will not be out-worked and I will not be out-prepared. Give me the rules. Define the playing field and the boundaries. Point out the goal or objective. I'll do the rest. Have I always won? No, but my mountains have far outnumbered my valleys.

The legendary Vince Lombardi once said, "The objective is to win: fairly, squarely, decently, win by the rules, but still win."[10] When people said I shouldn't or I couldn't, when they said I was the wrong guy because of my skin color—whatever they said, I viewed that as their problem, not mine. I was determined that if I signed up, I was going to win—fairly and squarely and by the rules—but to win.

ATTITUDE

Earlier in this chapter we briefly examined the debilitating effects of pessimism and chronic discouragement. Now let's consider the antidote.

Several years ago, picking up one of my sons at a basketball camp at the University of Oklahoma, I overheard Kelvin Sampson, the Sooners' head basketball coach at the time, telling the campers, "There are two things you can control. Your work ethic and your attitude." He was talking to the young basketball players, but it was a timely reminder to me as well. I've reminded myself of those words many times since then.

I'm talking about cultivating a positive mental attitude. I know, I know: just the phrase "positive mental attitude" can trigger groans in some people these days. They associate it with hyped-up motivational pep talks and old-fashioned lectures laced with quotations from Norman Vincent Peale. Nevertheless, your attitude has an immeasurable effect, for good or ill, on your life and the results you achieve. Your attitude isn't determined by anything outside of you. You choose your attitude. It comes from within.

Franco Harris, the running back for the Pittsburgh Steelers in their dynasty years of the 1970s, knew a little about cultivating a winning attitude. He owns four Super Bowl rings and was named to the Pro Bowl nine times. Franco once said: "How you look at a situation is very important, for how you think about a problem may defeat you before you ever do anything about it. When you get discouraged or depressed, try changing your attitude from negative to positive and see how life can change for you. Remember, your attitude toward a situation can help you to change it—you create the very atmosphere for defeat or victory."[11]

I've already mentioned that I arrived at OU assuming I was going to play right away. I obviously didn't lack confidence, but I needed the virtue of patience. What I did have was a basic desire to win. That attitude was nourished at OU and flourished at OU. The place resonated with a winning attitude, and it was contagious.

Confidence, as opposed to arrogance, and a positive outlook are the hallmarks of people who accomplish great things. Jimmy Johnson, the head coach of the Dallas Cowboys, set off a firestorm of criticism back in 1992 when he confidently predicted that his team would defeat the San Francisco 49ers in the NFC championship game and advance to the Super Bowl. At that point the Cowboys were only a few years removed from a 1–15 record in Johnson's second season as head coach, and they were enjoying their first winning season in seven years. Sportswriters around the country called him arrogant. Even in Dallas the local sports talk radio hosts dragged him over the coals for giving the 49ers incentive. When I heard Johnson's bold prediction, I mentally high-fived him for stoking a fire of expectancy within his team. What happened? The Cowboys not only beat San Francisco, they won the Super Bowl. They would go all the way two more times over the next three years.

Attitude determines altitude. I'm not sure who first said that, but he packed a mountain of truth into a three-word sentence. Most people live "under the circumstances." No matter what injustices, setbacks, or mistakes lie in your history, it's possible to rise above your circumstance. It's an unshakable biblical truth that your attitude has everything to do with your outcome in life.

By the way, there's no opting out of the law of attitude. It's working right now, either for you or against you. Your attitude is either propelling you toward success or dragging you toward failure. It is either causing you to press through adversity or to be stopped in your tracks. The important thing to know is that it's a choice! Remember, attitude determines altitude.

REFRAMING YOUR DESTINY

Letting God redeem your past. Cultivating persistence. Consistently giving maximum effort. Choosing a positive attitude. Nurturing an expectation of success. These are some of the tools I've used to keep my past from defining my future. They will work wonders for you too. Even if life has dealt you a difficult hand, you can rise above adversity and soar like an eagle.

If you don't believe me, I recommend a fifty-year-old book called *Cradles of Eminence* by the psychologists Victor and Mildred Goertzel, who examined the family backgrounds of three hundred exceptionally successful people.[12] The high achievers covered in the study included famous figures such as Franklin D. Roosevelt, Helen Keller, Winston Churchill, Albert Schweitzer, Mahatma Gandhi, and Albert Einstein as well as people who weren't household names but who had nonetheless accomplished extraordinary things.

The Goertzels' findings are inspiring and encouraging, especially for those who must contend with adversity or disadvantages. Here's how one reviewer summarized the Goertzels' results:

> Three-quarters of the children were troubled by poverty, a broken home, or by rejecting, over-possessive, or dominating parents. Seventy-four of the 85 writers of fiction or drama and 10 of the 20 poets came from homes where they saw tense psychological drama played out by their parents.
>
> Physical handicaps, such as blindness, deafness, or crippled limbs characterized over one-quarter of the sample. These people may have had more weaknesses and handicaps than many who had a healthy upbringing....[13]

Cradles of Eminence has been updated and expanded several times by Goertzel family members to cover more than seven hundred successful people. The basic message, however, is the same: You don't have to allow the past to determine the future. As Zig Ziglar puts it, "It's not what happens to you that determines how far you will go in life; it is how you handle what happens to you."[14]

God's principles for success and achievement are no respecters of persons. They will work for you no matter your race, background, social standing, or income. You cannot change what has happened to you in the past, but you can change your mindset. You can replace what holds you back in your old culture with new values and habits that are conducive to success.

Allow God to redeem your past and help you let go of hurts, guilt, and shame. Finding forgiveness and hope in Him, you can join the Apostle Paul in declaring, "One thing I do: forgetting what lies behind and reaching forward to what lies ahead, I press on toward the goal for the prize of the upward call of God in Christ Jesus."[15]

My faith has played a tremendous role in my determination to win. Faith encourages me to focus on facts and the truth of God's Word rather than what people say or how my circumstances appear.

Earlier I mentioned Norman Vincent Peale. The godfather of the motivational movement offered this summary of his life's message: "Four things for success: Work and pray. Think and believe." That's a pretty good recipe. Let's dig a little deeper into the power of the first ingredient in Peale's short list—work. It's not glamorous, but oh it is mighty.

CHAPTER 5

DIGGING DEEP FOR SELF-DISCIPLINE

Talent without discipline is like an octopus on roller skates. There's plenty of movement, but you never know if it's going to be forward, backwards, or sideways.

—H. Jackson Brown Jr.

I n the movie *The Natural*, a naïve young man from the country, seemingly custom-built by God Himself to excel at the game of baseball, makes a tragic moral mistake that shatters his major league dreams before they can take flight. After missing too many of his prime playing years, this gifted athlete finally gets his second-chance opportunity to play in "the bigs."

That was a fictional tale. Josh Hamilton's story is real. Coming out of high school in North Carolina, Hamilton appeared to have the natural tools to be one of the greatest baseball players in history. By the age of ten he was already hearing predictions that he would play major league baseball one day. In the years that followed, the boy, his skills, and his passion for the game all grew very, very large.

At Athens Drive High School in Raleigh, his near-fanatical dedication to baseball and training left no time for traditional teenage interests like dating, drinking, or parties. Josh was all baseball all the time. Meeting and sometimes exceeding those early predictions of baseball glory, Josh batted .556 his senior year and was the top high school prospect in the country in 1999. The Tampa Bay Devil Rays had the first pick that year and drafted him.

Josh's parents quit their jobs so they could accompany their teenage son on his climb up the ladder of the Rays' minor league system and, they hoped, to a spot on a major league roster within a year or two. That climb was going smoothly until an auto accident after a spring training game in 2001 injured all three of them, sending Josh's parents back to Raleigh to recuperate and keeping Josh off the field and out of the training room for the first time in his life. Suddenly the nineteen-year-old was a long way from home with too much time and money on his hands. He found himself spending day after day at a tattoo parlor with some new companions. "They weren't bad people," Josh later recalled. "They just did bad things."[1] Looking back, it's clear that Josh's first addiction was to ink. One tattoo led to another. And another. Soon the count was up to twenty-six.

With the encouragement of those "friends," Josh experienced his first drink of alcohol, first strip club, and first line of cocaine, all on the same night. Before long, bouts of binge drinking blurred the seemingly endless series of tattoos. Drinks were blended with drugs, and his "recreational" use of cocaine quickly mutated into an addiction to crack. Over the next few years, a series of failed drug tests and unsuccessful attempts at self-rehabilitation left Josh's dreams of baseball stardom in pieces.

His focus was no longer on the pursuit of baseball records. The pursuit of drugs now controlled his life. Josh described this nightmarish season of his life in frank and heartbreaking detail in a 2007 article for *ESPN Magazine* titled "I'm Proof that Hope Is Never Lost."[2] Homeless, emaciated, at rock bottom, Josh had a transformative encounter with Jesus Christ that put him on the road to recovery. It came, though, after too many of his prime playing years were lost, his body tragically diminished, the specter of relapse lurking in the shadows for the rest of his days on earth. In fact, he has relapsed more than once over the years.

The world will never know what heights Josh Hamilton might have reached in baseball. More to the point, *he* will never know. It's one of the oldest, saddest stories of them all and one of the most common—the tale of squandered talent, the tragedy of unrealized potential, the heartache and regret of missed opportunity. How many times have we seen it?

For me, one Oklahoma Sooner in particular comes to mind when I think about tragic, unrealized potential. Two seasons after I graduated from OU, a freshman burst onto the scene who seemed poised to become the next in Oklahoma's illustrious line of Heisman trophy running backs. Some thought this big, strong, lightning-fast kid out of Philadelphia, Mississippi, might surpass them all. He was that good. Twenty-seven years later, Marcus Dupree was the subject of an ESPN *30 for 30* documentary titled "The Best that Never Was."

That sad title says it all. Dupree was heavily recruited out of high school, but OU landed him. He started seeing playing time midway through his freshman season, electrifying the nation with a stunning combination of grace, speed, and power. In his first start, against Oklahoma State, he scored two touchdowns, continuing the season with a seventy-seven-yard punt return against Colorado, an eighty-yard run against Kansas State, a seventy-yarder versus Missouri, and an eighty-six-yard romp against archrival Nebraska. Despite not starting until the seventh game of the season, Dupree finished the regular season with 1,144 yards rushing and thirteen touchdowns. He was named second team All-American, first team all–Big Eight Conference, and Big Eight Newcomer of the Year.

At the end of the season, Oklahoma received an invitation to play Arizona State in the Fiesta bowl on January 1, but Dupree returned to practice after Christmas break fifteen pounds heavier and out of shape. Now, I've already bragged about my momma's cooking, but I don't think even she could have put fifteen pounds on me in a couple of weeks! Coach Switzer publicly voiced his concern and disappointment with Dupree's physical condition.

On New Year's night, in front of a national television audience, Dupree had to come out of the game on numerous offensive possessions because he was simply too winded to remain on the field. It's a testament to his immense natural gifts that after participating in only thirty-four offensive plays that night, he still accumulated 249 rushing yards—a

Fiesta Bowl record that stands to this day. After the game Coach Switzer told Dupree, "If you'd have been in shape, you'd have rushed for four hundred yards, and we'd have won the game."[3]

The following season, Dupree lasted four games before dropping out. He would resurface a few years later in a couple of attempts to play professional football, but it never worked out for him. He had mind-blowing ability, but he lacked the most important thing: the capacity for self-denial, also known as self-discipline.

I could cite many similar stories, especially from the world of sports, since great athletes have a high profile and perform on a very public stage. But the same sad pattern plays out in every area of human activity—the arts, business, academics, and government.

The gifted underachiever. The talented failure. The genius with the fatal inability to say no to some destructive habit or impulse. The prodigy who never learned how to delay gratification. You find this pattern everywhere, and too often we see it playing out in ourselves and in those we love.

Even people who from the outside appear to be quite successful can inwardly be aware they've left far too much on the table. Toward the end of George Bernard Shaw's life, an interviewer challenged the great playwright and critic to play the "What If" game. "Mr. Shaw," he began, "you have been around some of the most famous people in the world. You are on a first-name basis with royalty, world-renowned authors, artists, teachers, and dignitaries from every part of this continent. If you had your life to live over and could be anybody you've ever known, who would you want to be?" After pondering the question for a moment, Shaw replied, "I would choose to be the man George Bernard Shaw could have been, but never was."[4]

Have you ever heard more sobering words? Each of us is given one and only one life to live on this earth. No one should come to the end of it filled with regret about what he could have been.

I don't ever remember a time in my life when I wanted to be someone else. Growing up a Dallas Cowboys fan, I wanted to be *like* Roger Staubach, but I never wanted to *be* Roger Staubach. When I left Congress, I stepped back and took stock of my life and habits and didn't like what I saw. Even though I knew the biblical principles of digging deep for continual progress, I realized I had slipped in many areas. At that moment, I recommitted to becoming the best possible version of myself. I suspect you want that too.

Well, that simply isn't possible without the virtue of self-discipline. Unfortunately, this virtue has many enemies. Before we go on to examine some keys to harnessing the power of personal discipline, here are a few of the most notorious of those enemies.

SIX ENEMIES OF SELF-DISCIPLINE

1. YOUR FLESH

The first and most formidable of the enemies working to keep you from being the best possible version of yourself is what the Bible calls "the flesh." It refers to the cravings and impulses of our physical bodies in this fallen world.

One reason this is such a challenge is that we live in a land of abundance where instant gratification is more available to more people than at any time in history. Yes, I know these are hard times economically for many people and that lots of folks are struggling as they never have before. But *struggling* is a relative concept in twenty-first-century America. Most of us live like kings in comparison with most of the world. Come to think of it, we live like kings compared with *actual kings* from the past. I suspect that if you could exchange lives with a typical monarch from medieval or biblical times, you'd quickly miss indoor plumbing, hot showers, unspoiled meat, Google, the Internet, Andy Griffith reruns, key lime pie, and friends who brush their teeth.

Living in an age of comfort, convenience, and plenty is nice, but it exacts a price from us. If our bodies want something, we can have it. If our flesh gets an itch for something, we can scratch it quickly and easily. We crave and so we satisfy our craving. That's a dangerous way to live. Why? Because the flesh wants to run the show.

This is why self-discipline is one of the most important character traits a person can have. Its rarity in our world makes it all the more powerful. Possessing self-discipline is a competitive advantage. Yet what exactly is it?

It's the ability to put aside what we want *now* so we can achieve something higher and better *later*. It's the capacity to delay gratification in the pursuit of a greater goal. It's the willingness to dig deep and endure short-term pain for a long-term gain. Jesus called it denying yourself: "Then He said to them all, 'If anyone desires to come after Me, let him deny himself, and take up his cross daily, and follow Me.'"[5]

If we never deny ourselves, if we habitually obey the demands of our bodies and souls, we'll gradually lose the capacity to say no to ourselves at all. After a while, our appetites will dictate everything we do. In fact, the Apostle Paul once referred to people "whose god is their stomachs."[6] That certainly has been me at times. How about you?

It's interesting how we use our doctors today. Indulging the flesh produces symptoms. So we want our physician to give us a pill to deal with the symptoms so we can keep on indulging the flesh. We don't exercise. We don't follow nutritional wisdom because we want to continue stopping at the doughnut shop every time the "Hot Now" sign is illuminated. We don't find healthy ways to deal with daily stress. We just want the pill that enables us to keep on doing what we like doing. God designed our bodies to be our servants, not our masters. You see, we are all three-part persons. You have a body, you have a soul, and you have a spirit. Each part is fighting to be the boss.

A famous preacher once announced to a large crowd, "I have more trouble with D. L. Moody than any other man I've ever met."[7] Do you know who said that? D. L. Moody! I know exactly what he meant. I have more trouble with J. C. Watts Jr. than any other man I've met. Why? Because of the war within. My flesh says, "J. C., you don't really feel like working out today." But my mind and spirit say, "J. C., you've been traveling and haven't been in the gym for several days. You're losing momentum. Get your hind quarters onto that treadmill." Or the flesh says, "Go ahead and get that second piece of Italian cream cake or third piece of pie." The only reason there's a battle is because the flesh and its appetites are the enemy of the disciplines that lead to success.

2. PROCRASTINATION

"Later." It's probably the most common epitaph in the graveyard of dreams and goals. The late Victor Kiam, former owner of the New England Patriots, called procrastination "opportunity's assassin." Numerous studies have shown that people who chronically procrastinate are less healthy, less wealthy, and less happy than those with the self-discipline to be proactive.[8]

When we put off something important, it can feel like we're buying time, but the opposite is true. We're not buying it. We're spending it foolishly. Piers Steel describes a scene that's all too familiar: "We fritter away the days with the small pleasures of television and computer games, of Internet surfing and Sudoku puzzles and end up with nothing to show for it. This is a recipe for regret. In the short term, we regret what we do, but in the long term, we regret what we don't get done."[9]

Consistently putting off the *difficult* transforms it into the *impossible*. It's not a great strategy to put off building your ark until the rain clouds appear. You can't be both a procrastinator and self-disciplined. The vice is at war with the virtue.

3. RATIONALIZATION

Just this once won't hurt. No one will know. Every-body's doing it. I deserve this. I'll make up for it next time. It will never happen to me.

These are some of the common rationalizations we use. It's amazing what we're capable of rationalizing in the moment of temptation. When we really want to have something we shouldn't have or do something we shouldn't do, we can be pretty creative. This is why the habit of making rationalizations is a mortal enemy to self-discipline.

Each year many people are deceived and defrauded of millions of dollars by skillful con artists. Well, in a sense, when we rationalize, we are simply running a con game on ourselves. Our ability to deceive ourselves is impressive. In a survey, college professors were asked to evaluate their own teaching ability. A full 94 percent of them rated themselves as "above average." Now by definition, only 50 percent of those professors can actually be above average. In other words, a lot of them are fooling themselves.[10] We all do it. We sell ourselves the appealing but false idea that the principles God built into the universe don't apply to us. At least "not this one time."

It's easy to see how our human ability to rationalize threatens our self-discipline. Expert con men know the easiest lie to sell is the one the victim wants to believe. It is the same when we are conning ourselves. We tell ourselves:

"Cutting this corner won't make any difference."

"Skipping this step might be a problem for others, but not for me."

"Violating this principle won't come back to bite me."

"I'll double up later and make up for this."

"I can eat what I want and lose weight, because that's what the advertisement said."

None of this is true, but we believe these lies because we *want* them to be true. Like those over-confident college professors, we think we're more exceptional than we really are. We deceive ourselves into believing the rules don't apply to us, but they do.

4. RESISTANCE

In the late 1990s, I began experiencing something strange and upsetting. I had been a confident public speaker since my high school years, and in college I spoke to countless groups, large and small, including many church audiences.

I remember seeing a television interview with Florida State coach Bobby Bowden right before we played his team in the Orange Bowl my senior year. Coach Bowden and I had spoken at a Miami church the Sunday before the game. The reporter asked him what he thought about the Oklahoma quarterback they'd be facing. He said, "Well, I heard him speak the other day, and if he plays anything like he speaks, we're in trouble."

I never set out to be a public speaker. It was simply a part of the things I chose to do, like running for the Corporation Commission and later for Congress, which required giving countless speeches. I got accustomed to the challenge and became a decent speaker. I was surprised, then, when around the end of my first term in Congress, I suddenly began experiencing strange physical symptoms, especially before I was scheduled to speak to a small group. Shortness of breath and anxiety would sweep over me. I eventually learned, to my shock, that I was having a form of panic attack. This presented a serious challenge, obviously, for a politician, provoking a few embarrassing moments in my congressional leadership role and even once in a White House discussion with President George W. Bush.

I was faced with a choice: surrender to the disorder or fight it. Surrender could have meant not running for reelection to Congress and giving up much of the pastoral work that had been a part of my life. I chose to fight, taking encouragement from an article I read about the NFL Hall of Famer Earl Campbell. I was surprised to learn that he was blindsided by a severe version of an anxiety disorder shortly after he retired from professional football. With help, he found his way through it and pressed on. I did as well.

Nothing great is ever accomplished without pressing through resistance. What is resistance? On the physical level, it's the product of inertia, friction, and entropy. Inertia means that a body at rest wants to stay at rest. Once a body is moving, friction slows it down. And because of entropy, a body will eventually fall apart without constant attention and maintenance.

The laws of inertia, friction, and entropy apply to you and me. When the object at rest is you, you want to remain at rest. You'll have to overcome inertia to move forward. The good news is that once you get moving, inertia is your friend (more on this in a moment).

Committing yourself to achieving something great will produce friction between you and certain kinds of people around you. Not everyone will be cheering you on. Deciding to improve yourself will actually offend some people. Displaying self-discipline makes the undisciplined feel guilty.

Thanks to entropy, it's easier to tear things down than to build them up. In politics I found many people knew how to tear the house down but had no clue about how to build it back. Stop working out, and your conditioning will begin to deteriorate right away. Stop practicing a skill, and you'll quickly lose your edge.

The path of least resistance never leads to greatness. The resistance is strongest, in fact, along the path of greatest glory. In his short but inspiring book on the creative process, *Do the Work*, Steven Pressfield describes what a clever opponent resistance can be: "Resistance will tell you anything to keep you from doing your work. It will perjure, fabricate, falsify; seduce, bully, cajole. Resistance is protean. It will assume any form, if that's what it takes to deceive you. Resistance will reason with you like a lawyer or jam a nine-millimeter in your face like a stickup man. Resistance has no conscience. It will pledge anything to get a deal, then double-cross you as soon as your back is turned."[11]

If self-discipline came easily, everyone would be a high achiever. It isn't easy, and resistance is a major reason why.

5. FRAGMENTATION

We're scattered, constantly pulled in twenty different directions, bombarded by messages, information, and stimuli. The ping from our smartphone announcing a text or email has produced a special neurological reflex. We're the most distracted generation in history.

Technology keeps us in constant contact with our coworkers, customers, friends, and family. Smartphones give us instant access to vast storehouses of digitized information and entertainment from pretty much everywhere. All this access comes at a psychological cost. We're drowning in a sea of information, inundated by endless streams of electronic distraction, unable to concentrate, suffering from lost productivity, mental overload, and "brain fog."

It seems that life in the twenty-first century demands multi-tasking, but study after study shows that we humans are lousy at it. We're not built to multi-task. We're wired for focus.

This sort of fragmentation of our attention, energy, and passion is a major enemy of self-discipline. Zig Ziglar had this kind of fragmentation in mind when he wrote, "I don't care how much power, brilliance, or energy you have, if you don't harness it and focus it on a specific target, and hold it there, you're never going to accomplish as much as your ability warrants."[12]

Ziglar points to the sixth dangerous enemy of self-discipline when he tells us to focus "on a specific target." That target usually lies in the future, which means that we usually have to overcome the present.

6. THE PRESENT

The familiar phrase "Eat, drink, and be merry, for tomorrow we die" has been a rallying cry for several generations of partying young people. Ask the typical twenty-something American the origin of the phrase, and he'll probably tell you it's the title of a song by Usher or Justin Timberlake. In fact, it comes from the Bible. We find it there twice: Isaiah 22:13 and First Corinthians 15:32. In neither instance does the sentiment appear in a positive light. The prophet Isaiah admonishes a people that has been warned that a day of judgment is coming but, instead of sobering up, decides to continue the party. God shakes His head at His chosen people, who are literally living as if there were no tomorrow.

The Apostle Paul, insisting on the reality of the resurrection, declares to the Corinthians that this life is not all there is. There is an eternal existence beyond the grave, an existence that holds joyful rewards for some and bitter anguish for others. That's why he is willing to endure hardship in this life. If he didn't believe that with all his heart, he might as well indulge every desire of his flesh today!

Do you see the theme? When we lose sight of the future, when our sights are only on today, we lose the ability to deny our appetites and press through discomfort.

Thinking only of *now* robs us of our power to invest in *later*. We face a fierce battle because the present feels so very real, while the future exists only in our imaginations. It's not imaginary, though. The future always arrives, and when it does, most people are filled with regret because they haven't prepared. When tomorrow comes, they are not what they hoped to be or doing what they hoped to do because they didn't apply the necessary discipline "back then." As my favorite actor, Denzel Washington, once said, "I do the things I don't want to do so I can eventually do the things I want to do."

Well, we certainly have a lot of powerful enemies in the struggle for self-discipline. But don't be discouraged—we also have some formidable allies.

THE FIVE FRIENDS OF SELF-DISCIPLINE

Anyone can become a person of discipline. The principles and laws God set in place when He made the world don't discriminate on the basis of age, race, sex, or background. They will work for everyone. As we just saw in the previous section, they will also work against us. The choice is ours.

If you want to maximize your potential and enjoy the fulfillment of stepping into your destiny, you'll need to put the following principles to work on your behalf every day.

1. SETTING GOALS: EYES ON THE PRIZE

The 1957 World Series, played about six weeks before I was born, pitted the mighty New York Yankees against the upstart Milwaukee Braves. Both rosters featured young home-run hitters who would go on to be legends of the game: Mickey Mantle for the Yankees and Hank Aaron for the Braves. One of the thrills of my congressional career was meeting Hank Aaron, and Mickey Mantle was from my home state of Oklahoma.

In Game Four, the Yankees were leading the series two games to one. Yogi Berra, behind home plate for New York, was known for constantly chattering in hopes of distracting or getting into the heads of opposing batters. Did you think trash talking was a recent invention? The Yankees were up 1–0 in the fourth inning when Hank Aaron came to the plate with two runners on base. Berra, sensing trouble, ramped up his efforts to get inside Aaron's head. "Hey, Henry, you're holding the bat wrong," Berra told him. "You're supposed to hold it so you can read the trademark." Aaron didn't blink or say a word, but when the next pitch was delivered he sent it over the left-field wall and into the seats. After rounding the bases and tagging home plate, Aaron looked at Berra and calmly said, "I didn't come up here to read."[13] The Braves won that game in extra innings and went on to win the World Series.

Henry David Thoreau observed, "In the long run men hit only what they aim at." It's true. The power of goal-setting has been documented so completely and emphasized so frequently over the years that it almost seems unnecessary to mention it. Yet surveys and my personal experience coaching others show that remarkably few people actually take the step of establishing and writing down their goals. My wife and I have been married for thirty-eight years, and she can vouch for the fact that I have been writing down my goals and backing them up with pictures on walls, in prayer rooms, on refrigerators, and in notebooks for at least thirty-five years.

Goal-setting really does carry supernatural power. Andrew Carnegie was the wealthiest man in America when he said, "If you want to be happy, set a goal that commands your thoughts, liberates your energy, and inspires your hopes."[14] To people on the outside looking in, setting bold goals can appear cocky or arrogant. In fact, appropriate goals probably should look that way to outsiders. If yours don't, maybe you're shooting too low.

When the future Heisman Trophy winner and NFL Hall of Famer Roger Staubach arrived at the United States Naval Academy, his reputation as a talented quarterback preceded him. The Midshipmen's backup QB, aware that Staubach was the incoming competition, thought he'd subject the plebe to a little verbal hazing. "Hey, Staubach!" he barked at breakfast one Sunday, "I hear you're going to take my job away. Is that right?"

"No, sir," replied Roger.

The upperclassman pressed the issue. "That's strange," he said. "I'm sure that's what I heard."

"What is your job, sir?" asked Roger.

"Number two quarterback," the upperclassman announced.

"I can assure you, I will not be taking your job away, sir," Roger assured him. The upperclassman was walking away when Roger added, "It's the starting quarterback job that I'm going to take, sir." And he did.

Writing down specific, measurable goals may be the most widely known and widely ignored piece of advice for self-improvement. Notice that I say *specific* and *measurable*. Without those two characteristics, your goal is really a wish. "I want to lose weight" is a wish. "I will lose fifteen pounds over the next three months" is a goal. In other words, goals clearly state *how much* and *by when*.

So what does goal-setting have to do with self-discipline? Well, say you've been undisciplined in your spending, and as a result your finances are a mess. Setting a goal of being completely debt free by a certain date and keeping that goal constantly before you can have a powerful effect on your spending choices in the moment of temptation. By keeping your eyes on the prize, you'll eliminate self-defeating choices and behavior. Setting a detailed goal and keeping it constantly before you also neutralizes the enemy of fragmentation I described earlier.

Goal-setting helps you achieve self-discipline, but the street runs both ways. In other words, as you cultivate the quality of self-discipline, you'll be able to achieve more goals, more quickly.

2. FEEDBACK: THE LAW OF KEEPING SCORE

Fitness trackers are everywhere. Even if you're not wearing one right now, you almost certainly know people who are. Most of them come in the form of a wristband, but some can be clipped to a shirt pocket or collar. A new generation of "smart watches" all arrive with built in fitness tracking capabilities. They tell you how many steps you've taken, how far you've run and how fast, how many calories you've expended, and how much you tossed and turned in the night. Some can even encourage you to relax when your stress levels rise too high. These popular devices not only help wearers know how much they've done but actually motivate them to do more, operating on the simple but powerful principle of *feedback*. Once you get consistent reports about how many steps you've taken so far in your day, you'll find ways to take more. We're hardwired to respond to feedback.

Feedback is deployed in a multitude of ways to modify our behavior. You may have noticed more and more of those radar boxes that tell you how fast you're driving on certain streets in your city. Wherever these boxes have been deployed, they have brought down the average speed of drivers. This happens even though everyone knows that the boxes merely report your speed, which you can learn from a glance at your speedometer; they don't enforce the speed limit. The signs, reports *Wired* magazine, "leverage what's called a feedback loop, a profoundly effective tool for changing behavior. The basic premise is simple. Provide people with information about their actions in real time (or something close to it), and then give them an opportunity to change those actions, pushing them toward better behaviors. Action, information, reaction."[15]

Simply being reminded of something consistently is an encouragement to do more of it, if it's a good thing, or less of it, if it's harmful. On the other hand, out of sight, out of mind. If you don't know how many calories you've consumed today, you're unlikely to give it a thought, much less care.

In every football game I ever played, my team had a powerfully motivating feedback device: the scoreboard. As a quarterback I glanced at it regularly. I needed to know not only the score but down and distance and the time remaining. Few things focus your mind like seeing that you're down by six points with less than three minutes to play.

It's easy to focus on your weight because you get feedback every morning, even if you never step onto a scale. It's called putting on your pants. A tightening pair of trousers is an unavoidable signal that you're putting on pounds. Consistent feedback loops—focusing our attention, motivating us, holding us accountable—are a powerful tool for cultivating discipline. You can't tell if you're winning if you don't keep score.

3. STARTING: THE LAW OF MOMENTUM

"The secret of getting ahead is getting started," said Mark Twain. It's true. I once heard someone ask an experienced fitness trainer the secret of getting motivated to exercise. If he expected to hear about an esoteric method of mind control, he was disappointed. The trainer's answer was simply "Start." He went on to explain that once a person starts to exercise, he likes the way he feels, so he wants to keep going. The reason most people don't exercise is that they never start.

Whether he knew it or not, this trainer was describing the law of momentum. Just as an object at rest wants to remain at rest, an object in motion wants to remain in motion. The law of momentum applies to every area of life, and when you're trying to become a disciplined high achiever, it's especially powerful.

Lots of people talk about what they want to do. I hear them all the time. Almost everyone daydreams of a better life and great accomplishments. Many even make detailed plans. Very few *act*, and that is the primary difference between the rare few who scale the heights in their chosen fields. Jack Canfield, co-creator of the motivational *Chicken Soup for the Soul* books, says that the successful people he has met and studied over the years tend to have what he calls "a bias for action."[16] Disciplined people take action, and action aids self-discipline.

People with a perfectionist bent often get trapped in what I call *perfectionist paralysis*. If you wait until conditions are ideal, you'll never start. Conditions are never ideal. You'll always find a reason to wait. Steven Pressfield warns against this tendency: "Don't prepare. Begin. Remember, our enemy is not lack of preparation; it's not the difficulty of the project or the state of the marketplace or the emptiness of our bank account. The enemy is Resistance. The enemy is our chattering brain, which, if we give it so much as a nanosecond, will start producing excuses, alibis, transparent self-justifications, and a million reasons why we can't/shouldn't/won't do what we know we need to do. Start before you're ready."[17]

W. Clement Stone, who founded the Combined Insurance Company at the age of seventeen and built it into a billion-dollar enterprise, used to give every new salesman a large bronze medallion inscribed with three short words: "Do it now!" Stone instilled a bias for action. Each salesman was to keep that medallion in his pocket at all times. Any time he was wavering about whether to pick up the phone or knock on a door, he was to reach into his pocket and feel that medallion, which would remind him of the power of taking action. This simple device worked for thousands of Combined salespeople over the years, turning many into great successes. It was said that the medallions of the most successful agents were worn completely smooth from years of reaching into their pockets and rubbing their fingers across that simple reminder—"Do it now!"

Start. Crawl, walk, run, but get moving. The old saying is no less true for being endlessly repeated: The journey of a thousand miles begins with a single step. Take that step and get the law of momentum working for you.

4. FUEL: THE LAW OF PASSION

Many people mistakenly believe that if they have a particular calling, they will always feel happy and excited working at it. That simply isn't the case.

Excelling in any area means dealing with *the grind*. When we see someone perform with consummate skill— whether in music, art, craftsmanship, sales, athletics, or entrepreneurship—it's easy to assume that his virtuosity comes naturally. What we don't see is the thousands of hours of sweat and diligence and practice and preparation that went into making his performance look so effortless. What pulled him through those lonely hours? Passion. Desire. Enthusiasm.

Several years ago I was invited by the U.S. Olympic Committee to speak to athletes about representing America abroad. It was a thrill to have the likes of LeBron James, Kobe Bryant, Dwayne Wade, and Dwight Howard in my audience. I'll never forget Coach Mike Krzyzewski's telling me afterward about Kobe Bryant's work ethic. Disciplining himself to pay the price mentally and physically, Kobe pushed himself to improve and excel. Athletes like Kobe make it look easy, but trust me, they work at it.

You can't avoid hard work if you're going to get where you want to go. That's why knowing how to stoke the fires of desire and enthusiasm is essential. Ralph Waldo Emerson wrote, "Enthusiasm is one of the most powerful engines of success. When you do a thing, do it with all your might. Put your whole soul into it. Stamp it with your own personality. Be active, be energetic and faithful, and you will accomplish your object. Nothing great was ever achieved without enthusiasm."[18]

Passion is linked to desire. Some people have been brainwashed by a culture of failure into thinking there's something wrong with ambition, that the only admirable person is a victim. I know highly successful people who started in public housing. I've also seen people from public housing stay in public housing. By the same token, I've seen people from uptown achieve great success, but many don't. In each case, the difference is ambition.

In many neighborhoods, and especially black neighborhoods, you'll encounter the poisonous attitude that someone who starts at the bottom and through hard work and diligence makes it to the top is somehow illegitimate, that he's forgotten where he came from, that he's no longer "authentic" or "authentically black." The implication is that rather than earning what he's accomplished, someone gave it to him because he "sold out." In too many urban schools, the idea has taken hold that if a student really wants to apply himself to learning and succeed in academics, he is trying to "act white" and is socially ostracized for it.[19] Such a concept would have made the Reverend Martin Luther King and the pioneers of the civil rights movement weep tears of disbelief. I will be the first to say that I'm not a self-made man. Many people have helped me along the way. But I applaud and will defend anyone accepting a hand out or a hand up who works hard to succeed.

5. FUTURE: THE LAW OF VISION

While a fixation on the present moment can be a mortal enemy of self-discipline, a clear vision of the future you hope to enjoy can be self-discipline's greatest ally. That vision—a clear sense of higher purpose—makes it possible to endure the short-term pain.

Stephen Covey relates a powerful insight by the Austrian psychologist Viktor Frankl, a survivor of Auschwitz and Dachau. Wondering why some persons survived the Nazi death camps and some did not, Frankl, a keen observer of human behavior, made a startling discovery:

> He looked at several factors—health, vitality, family structure, intelligence, and survival skills. Finally he concluded that none of these factors was primarily responsible. The single most significant factor, he realized, was a sense of future vision, the compelling conviction of those who were to survive that they had a mission to perform, some important work left to do.
>
> Survivors of POW camps in Vietnam and elsewhere have reported similar experiences: a compelling, future-oriented vision is the primary force that kept many of them alive.[20]

Senator John McCain was one of those prisoners of war, enduring years of confinement and torture in the Hanoi Hilton. I served in Congress with Senator McCain and am proud to know him. In fact, despite a few political disagreements, he's one of my heroes. When you shake his hand, you feel the sacrifice he made.

Here's my point. The same force that can pull someone through the hellish adversity of a concentration camp or a POW camp can certainly pull you and me through any obstacles and resistance we encounter. That force is a future-oriented vision, a sense of purpose or calling. It's a clear inner picture of who you want to become and what you will be doing ten, twenty, thirty years from now. The more vivid and detailed that picture, the more power it will have to propel you forward.

If you don't have a clear picture of the person you're called to be in the future, how can you know whether the things you're investing your time and effort in are moving you closer to being that person? As the Roman statesman Seneca observed, "To the person who does not know where he wants to go, there is no favorable wind."

Each of these tools—setting goals, feedback, starting, fuel, and future vision—will assist you in your battle for self-discipline and self-improvement. Combined, they make an amazing team.

Why is self-discipline so vital? Because, as a wise man once said, "If we don't discipline ourselves, the world will do it for us."[21] Life tends to be hard on those who do whatever they please. The Bible's wisdom book, Proverbs, is filled with warnings to "fools" and "sluggards" and those who refuse to acknowledge the principles upon which God founded creation. My grandmother used to speak of "being out there on Fool's Hill." She meant not taking the wisdom of Proverbs and applying it.

INSTEAD OF JUST STRUGGLING TO SAY NO, BUILD A MORE POWERFUL YES

Simply trying to maintain the willpower to say no every day to the things that undermine your future is a losing strategy. You have to develop a "yes" that out-weighs and out-pulls the "no" in your life.

That "yes"—your dream, your vision, your God-given purpose for being on the earth—will fuel all the work and sacrifice required to make it a reality. You can be sure, it *will* require work. I can attest to that.

As I've mentioned previously, I was never the biggest, the fastest, the strongest, or the most naturally gifted, but I always did know how to work hard. Neither my education nor my pedigree qualified me to do or accomplish some of the things I've been able to do. I've discovered that's the way it is with most people who achieve. Background, advantage, and privilege don't correlate to achievement. Hard work and determination do.

That's why you should never allow anyone—government bureaucrats, politicians, Republicans, Democrats, self-anointed leaders, talking heads, or the conventional wisdom crowd—to define you. You must not let them tell you who you are or what you can or can't do. They'll certainly try. If you are from a poor background, all the above will tell you that you can't succeed. If you're from a wealthy background, they will tell you that you can. "They" are frequently wrong on both counts.

It's not about where you started. It's about where you end up, and that is largely determined by your hold on seemingly old-fashioned values like determination, education, willingness to be taught, sacrifice, commitment, hard work, and, of course, the grace of God. All the bad statistics you hear about in different neighborhoods? That was me without the grace of God.

Let me close this chapter by pointing out that it's possible to succeed at the temporal level and still fail at the spiritual level. Spiritual success is the most important kind. It's what makes the other kinds of success eternally meaningful.

As with every other form of success, growing spiritually requires work. In contrast, going the way this fallen world says I should go takes no work at all. It is the path of least resistance. There is no struggle required to respond to injustice the way my flesh wants to respond. It's easy to respond in kind when others treat me unfairly or unkindly.

It takes effort to swim against the tide of our self-destructive, spiritually bankrupt culture. In the recipe for your success—the formula that turns you into the very best possible version of who God created you to be—there is an irreplaceable ingredient. It is *work*: working every day, peeling the pages of Scripture, digging deeper to understand and gain knowledge concerning the principles of Christ.

Working hard is essential. Working harder and *smarter* is even better. That's the next stop on our journey into digging deep.

CHAPTER 6

GO SMART. BE SMART.

I do not think much of a man who is not wiser today than he was yesterday.

—Abraham Lincoln

I n the musical adaptation of the film *The Color Purple*, the central character, Celie, who has grown older and wiser through adversity, sings,

Got my eyes. Though they don't see as far now,
They see more 'bout how things really are now.[1]

When I heard those lines, they struck a chord in my soul, expressing something I'd been feeling for a while, especially since becoming a grandfather, getting a little "snow on my rooftop," and being forced to keep a pair of reading glasses with me at all times. I've realized that with the years and the experiences I've had—some of which I've shared in this book—I've accumulated some insights about how to dig deeper and "do life better." I certainly don't know everything. Far from it. I'm also not fully walking in the wisdom I have managed to acquire. I frequently fall short in many areas because of my fleshly pride.

Yet even as my eyesight gets more challenged, I see many things more clearly now about Democrats and Republicans, business, grace, forgiveness, and even the church. As one of the wisest men who ever lived once wrote:

> Don't turn your back on wisdom, for she will
>   protect you.
> Love her, and she will guard you.
> Getting wisdom is the wisest thing you can do!
> And whatever else you do, develop good judg-
>   ment.
> If you prize wisdom, she will make you great.
> Embrace her, and she will honor you.[2]

SMART CHOICES

In other words, go smart and be smart. To be specific, there are six areas of life in which the choices you make will largely determine what you experience, what you achieve, and what kind of legacy you leave when your race is finished. It's important to choose wisely.

1. BE SMART ABOUT RELATIONSHIPS AND ASSOCIATIONS

"He fell in with the wrong crowd."

"She fell in love with the wrong kind of guy."

How often you hear about someone with talent, promise, and potential who, by getting mixed up with the wrong people, ended up a statistic instead of a success. Stories like Josh Hamilton's are all too familiar. Your choice of associates, friends, and mentors can work for you or against you. If you surround yourself with people whose lives are pointing the direction you hope to go, you'll experience lift, not drag.

Some people seem to bring out the worst in us. Others tend to bring out our best. Our choice of teammates affects nearly everything we do. It matters whom we listen to, whom we hang out with, and whom we allow to speak into our lives. The best teammates challenge you to improve. They hold you accountable. They encourage you when you're down and call you out when you're slacking off or being a knucklehead.

The book of Proverbs tells us, "Faithful are the wounds of a friend, but the kisses of an enemy are deceitful."[3] Cedrick Brown, a former defensive back for the Philadelphia Eagles and now a pastor, paraphrases that verse like this: "It is always better to have a friend to tell you what you *need* to hear rather than what you *want* to hear."[4] Be smart about whom you allow to have influence in your life.

Letting only the right people influence you doesn't mean you shouldn't try to be a good influence on people who are struggling or making bad choices. We shouldn't throw people away or write them off as hopeless cases. No one's life loses its value because of the mistakes he's made, as Pastor Joel Osteen illustrates strikingly: "Take a crisp new dollar bill in your hands. What is the value of that piece of paper? 'One dollar,' of course. Now take that bill and wad it up, throw it in the dirt, stomp on it a few times, run over it with your car, and then spill some mustard on it. Now what is the value of that crumpled, ragged, stained, and disfigured bill? Its purchasing power remains 'one dollar.' Its value has not diminished even though it has been abused and marred by misuse."

The same is true of you and me and everyone you meet. Each one of us has enormous value in God's eyes, and nothing we've done or has been done to us changes that. Whether our wounds are inflicted by others or ourselves, we still matter to God. A person doesn't depreciate like a car. That's why we must never write anyone off. How many times have we heard the story of a shipwrecked life completely turned around because a caring person reached out in unconditional love?

Many people have lost hope. They've come to believe they are disqualified to make something of their lives. We have to show them they're wrong. That begins by showing them they're not invisible to us. The inmate in jail or the one just released, the unwed teenage mom, the alcoholic, the drug addict—God loves them too. Christian leadership should run *to* them not *from* them. Far too often we "see through" people with problems because we lack a heart to see them through.

God knows I've made my share of boneheaded choices, coming dangerously close on occasion to becoming a statistic. I've also had good people of every race and walk of life sow seeds of encouragement and wisdom in my life. They invested in me and asked nothing in return. As a result, I've never felt disqualified to go for the gold, even when I might have encountered racial prejudice. I owe that confidence to good teachers, coaches, parents, pastors, friends, and an exceedingly wise grandmother who faced many more hurtful obstacles than I can even imagine.

Building that confidence in young people takes moms and dads, friends, churches, and teachers—real people engaged personally in their lives, showing them what a productive member of society looks like, making sure they know that success isn't an accident of birth but the product of certain attitudes and values.

For the same reasons, we need to wisely choose mentors and friends who model and remind us of those same truths.

2. BE SMART ABOUT MONEY

A nineteenth-century Scottish theologian observed, "A man's treatment of money is the most decisive test of his character—how he makes it and how he spends it."[5] I agree. You have to approach wealth, material things, and debt in the right way if you're going to do life better, but it's precisely this area of life that so many of us get wrong.

For some people money is like a drug; no matter how much they get they need more. For some it's a means of instant gratification for every impulse or itch. For some it's compensation for their insecurities, believing outward wealth somehow imparts inward value. For others it's an idol, commanding their worship and devotion. For many, it's an elusive messiah. Such people believe that money will solve their problems. They're all mistaken. Our brokenness isn't in our bank accounts. It's in our souls.

Money makes a tragically poor substitute for God, but it is not, as many people seem to believe, inherently bad. Misquoting Paul, they say, "Money is the root of all evil," whereas the apostle actually wrote, "The *love of* money is the root of all evil."[6] God created material goods to serve man, not man to serve material goods.

We have to reject what I call a "poverty mentality." This is the idea, popular in some Christian circles, that God is against your having anything in this life, as if to say, "Yes, you'll enjoy heaven by and by, but until you get there, you're destined to barely scrape by, and if you do start experiencing some success, then you're obviously doing something wrong and need to repent." This is twisted theology. Jimmy Evans of the MarriageToday ministry says, "Satan wants us broke and broken." God is not against your having things. He is against things having you.

Being smart about money means first of all understanding that merely accumulating money shouldn't be the primary objective. The goal should be true *prosperity*, encompassing not only finances, but every area of life: relationships, health, work, and community. The prosperous person thrives in spirit, soul, and body.

Yet most people think the only thing they lack to make them happy is sufficient money. "Man tends to think he's merely *incomplete* when his problem is he's *incorrect*," as Pastor Creflo Dollar says. By "incorrect" he means that brokenness we all have on the inside, which only a relationship with God through Jesus Christ can begin to repair. More money won't fix that. I could fill a long shelf with books packed with examples of people who suddenly came into great wealth—through winning a lottery or making it big in sports, business, or entertainment—and it ruined them.

Money couldn't complete them. They weren't incomplete. They were incorrect.

We live in a culture in which an unprecedented number of households are living under crushing, unsustainable loads of credit card debt, accumulated in a desperate effort to satisfy their inward hunger with money and things. It's been said that we buy things we don't need with money we don't have to impress people we don't like. We try to keep up with the Joneses, and just when we think we've caught them, they refinance.

Sadly, the same is true of our government. We're saddling future generations of Americans with debt and transfer payment obligations that they'll never be able to pay. Republicans and Democrats are responsible for this. The Chamber of Commerce crowd will pounce on any Republican or Democrat who doesn't vote to raise the debt limit, yet there's not one member of the chamber that would allow its balance sheet to show debt running at six times revenue. You can't out-exercise a bad diet, and you can't outgrow a bad budget or bad policies.

We have to be on guard against making wealth an idol. Idolatry no longer involves bowing down and sacrificing to some lifeless statue. We commit idolatry by looking to anyone or anything other than God for meaning, fulfillment, and happiness, and it is seductively easy to start doing that with money. Man is hardwired to worship. It isn't an option. We will make *something* an object of our worship, whether it's God or some poor, toxic substitute. That's idolatry.

The best defense against idolatry is cultivating a heart of generosity toward God and others. Giving is the key to experiencing true prosperity. Generosity is less difficult if we realize that everything we have comes from and belongs to God. This is the fundamental principle of stewardship. As pastor Robert Morris points out in his eye-opening book *The Blessed Life*,

> It is all God's and we merely exercise stewardship over it. When we get God's perspective on money—when we understand that God owns it all—it is easy to give it when He asks for it. We give it to Him freely and we don't grieve over it. We understand that it wasn't ours in the first place.
>
> Whenever I observe a Christian operating selfishly, I know I'm looking at a person who either doesn't know or has forgotten that it all belongs to God. They are acting like an owner, not a steward.[7]

Why did God create giving? To deal with selfishness and greed. God doesn't need your money, but if God can get us to deal with selfishness, unforgiveness, pride, greed, lust, and ego, he will get our money.

Going smart with your money means operating with practical, biblical wisdom in your finances, generosity to others, prudence with debt, delaying gratification. Most of all it means keeping money in its proper place in your heart and mind—ever mindful that wealth is a blessing that allows you to bless others.

3. BE SMART ABOUT TIME

Just as we are stewards of the wealth we control, we are also stewards of the hours we are given in each new day. You and I, Bill Gates and the guy sleeping in a cardboard box beneath the overpass—we all have twenty-four hours every day to use in any way we choose. The Christian writer Richard Gaylord Briley says, "Time is neither our friend nor our enemy; it is something that gets measured out to us to see what we will make of it."[8]

Time is more precious than money because of its scarcity. Wealth can be created. Time cannot. Wisdom in managing our time, therefore, is essential to doing life better. And there have never been more demands and opportunities to distract us than we face today. The question is how to get the most *important* things done with so many *urgent* yet ultimately unimportant things competing—*shouting*—for our attention? The answer is setting and honoring priorities.

In *First Things First*, Stephen Covey tells a story about a group of high-powered over-achievers assembled for a seminar on time management. Announcing a quiz, the instructor produces a wide-mouthed gallon jar, into which he places, one by one, several fist-sized rocks. When no more rocks will fit, he asks, "Is this jar full?" The class says yes, to which he responds, "Really?" Pulling out a bucket, he pours gravel into the jar, shaking it until the pebbles settle into the spaces between the larger rocks. Smiling, the instructor asks, "Now is the jar full?" By this time the class is on to him. "Probably not," one of them answers. "Good!" he replies, pulling out a bucket of sand, which he pours into the spaces left between the rocks and the gravel. Once more he asks, "Is this jar full?"

"No!" the class shouts, and the instructor pours water in until the jar is filled to the brim. Then he looks up at the class and asks, "Can anyone tell me what the point of this illustration is?" One eager beaver raises his hand and says, "The point is, no matter how full you think your schedule is, you can always fit some more things into it!"

"No," the instructor replies, "that's not the point. The truth this illustration teaches us is: If you don't put the big rocks in first, you'll never get them in at all."[9]

We say yes to every little demand and every opportunity and then wonder why the most important things never get done. No matter what your calling, there are some "big rock" things you should be doing in order to progress toward your goal. We all have some of the same big rocks—church, prayer, exercise, and investment in our most important relationships—which are essential to being healthy in spirit, soul, and body. Yet these are the very things that tend to get pushed out of our week by less important yet seemingly more urgent tasks. I have come to understand this principle much better in the last ten years. I can't accept every invitation or campaign for every candidate or every important cause. As much as I'd like to, I just don't have the space in my jar.

It all comes down to scheduling your big rocks in advance and then respecting your schedule. If you don't respect the priorities of your schedule, how can you expect anyone else to do so?

Bill Hybels, the influential pastor of Willow Creek Community Church and the author of *Simplify: Ten Practices to*

Unclutter Your Soul, speaks often of building your schedule around who you want to become, not what you need to accomplish.[10] For example, if you want to be a healthier, fitter person one year from now, you will put your workouts on your schedule in ink and make them sacred.

Ten years ago I decided to pay more attention to my health and devote more time to prayer and contemplation. Knowing that at the end of the day I'm just too spent to exercise or pray well, I started scheduling my workouts and quiet time early in the morning. If you want to be a better parent, you will put quality time with your children on your schedule instead of giving them the leftovers. If you want to learn a foreign language, you'll put study sessions on your calendar and protect them. Strategic scheduling, says Pastor Hybels, "was one of the greatest simplifying revelations of my life. When you put a schedule together, and before you list all the duties and responsibilities, you say, 'Who do I want to become in the next 12 months?' You plug in the time it'll take you; you fill in the rest with what you have to get done. If that subtle shift can be made, you can be helped in dramatic ways."[11]

In the fifth chapter of his letter to the Ephesians, the Apostle Paul declares the value of going smart with your time management: "So be careful how you live. Don't live like fools, but like those who are wise. Make the most of every opportunity in these evil days."[12] Look around—we too live in "evil days." All the more reason to make every day count. As the novelist Arnold Bennett wrote, "We shall never have more time. We have, and always had, all the time there is."[13]

4. BE SMART ABOUT YOUR NAME

Raymond Donovan, President Ronald Reagan's first secretary of labor, was forced to resign in 1985 when he was indicted on charges that many suspected were politically motivated. He faced months of withering adverse publicity, but when the case finally came to trial, Donovan was quickly acquitted of all the charges. In an impromptu news conference following the verdict, Donovan famously demanded, "Which office do I go to to get my reputation back?"[14] I too know the terrible pain of seeing your good name tarnished in the media and being powerless to do anything about it.

From my youngest days my parents taught me to cultivate and protect a reputation for integrity. Having stumbled a few times, I can identify with the psalmist David when he pleads with the Lord, "Remember not the sins of my youth."[15] Those missteps would be much worse if they happened today, when social media can dismantle in an afternoon a reputation for integrity and excellence that took years to build. Never has the old adage been more timely, "A lie can travel halfway around the world before the truth can get its pants on." In the age of the Internet, everything lives forever. Google never forgets.

We don't always get a say in what happens *to* us or what is said *about* us, but what we can control is keeping our word. That's not always easy to do, as I was reminded in 2001, when I was still serving in Congress. After committing to speak to an audience of Boy Scouts in Oklahoma City, I received a special invitation to a White House reception for the newly crowned national champion Oklahoma

Sooners football team—on the same date as my speech to the Scouts. Let me tell you, that was one reception I was dying to attend, so I asked about getting the date changed. To my deep disappointment, I was told it wasn't possible.

The only way I could be at the White House reception was to cancel on the Scouts, but I couldn't bring myself to disappoint them. Yes, it would have been a thrill, as a former OU quarterback, to join the Sooner champions for a photo and celebration with the president of the United States, but I wanted the Scouts to know that I thought their sacrifice, citizenship, and hard work was important to me, even if it meant missing a once-in-a-lifetime opportunity. I also wanted those young men to see commitment modeled by someone in public office.

As important as it is to have a good name in the marketplace and in the professional world, it's even more important to be known for keeping your word at home. Our spouses and our children need to know they can count on us no matter what. We can become so consumed with making a living that we fail to make a life, with trying to be a hero to people we don't even know that we miss opportunities to be a hero to those closest to us. I've been as guilty as anyone on this score at times, but occasionally I've gotten it right. When I showed up for my seven-year-old son's flag football game on the evening of my reelection to Congress in 1998, the other parents were shocked to see me there, but I wanted my son to know that his game was as important to me as my campaign watch party.

Some things are beyond your control, but it pays off in the long run when you do everything you can to be known as a person of character. We all have done things we would like to take back, and unfortunately some people may hold those mistakes against us for the rest of our lives. But a person who follows through on a commitment, who under-promises and over-delivers, who consistently treats others as he desires to be treated will reap the dividends. As Solomon wrote, "A good name is to be more desired than great wealth."[16]

5. BE SMART ABOUT APPROVAL AND FAME

Having spent my entire adult life performing before huge audiences, first as a football player and then in politics and on the speakers' circuit, I've learned that the roar of the crowd is one of the most powerful drugs on earth, delivering an intoxicating rush that is addictive. If you're not careful, hunger for that kind of affirmation can drive everything you do. Entertainers can be some of the most fragile and insecure people you will ever meet, deeply dysfunctional men and women who feel whole and important only when they're on stage in the spotlight. When their season of popularity ends—as it inevitably does—they can feel worthless and lost. The great R&B singer Anita Baker told an interviewer, "Applause felt like approval, and it became a drug that soothed the pain, but only temporarily."[17] Lady Gaga graphically described the narcotic effect of adulation in her song "Applause": "If only fame had an IV.../ I found the vein, put in here / I live for the applause...."

The danger is there for all of us, even those who do not perform before thousands. We're all susceptible to the seductive pull of acceptance by the "in crowd." This is the nature of peer pressure, which is by no means a problem only for young people. We face it throughout life, in the workplace and in the marketplace. The most intense peer pressure I've ever seen was not in high school but in Congress, where the pressure to go along to get along is incredible.

Trying to satisfy a powerful need for applause is a precarious way to live. If you can be elevated by praise you're vulnerable to being crushed by criticism. If you can't function without affirmation from others, you give them a power over you they weren't meant to have. Most importantly, when you face a crisis in which you can either stand on principle or compromise with the world, you will fold like a lawn chair.

So what is the answer? It is developing confidence in who you are in God, realizing who He made you to be and what He has called you to do, understanding that He has made and accepts you wholly and unconditionally. The Apostle Paul encouraged the believers of Ephesus to set aside people-pleasing and to concentrate on impressing an audience of One: "Work with enthusiasm, as though you were working for the Lord rather than for people."[18] Often in life—and especially in politics—people love you because of who you are, but God loves us in spite of who we are.

Only two opinions ultimately matter—yours and God's. You have to look yourself in the mirror every morning, and one day you'll have to stand before God as you prepare to enter eternity. Why on earth would you allow the fickle, misguided, uninformed opinions of others to determine your sense of worth or your direction?

I have an independent streak, as my colleagues in Congress learned. If I hadn't known who I was, what I believed, and what God put me on this earth to do, I never could have taken unpopular stands or bucked the system. I would have done what so many in life end up doing—going with the flow and thinking with the crowd.

Being smart about approval and the praise of others means appreciating affirmation when it comes without enjoying it so much that it becomes a need rather than a blessing. I once heard it said that flattery is like perfume. You should smell it and not drink it.

6. BE SMART ABOUT PEOPLE, GOD, AND GOVERNMENT

God is God. The government isn't. Neither are you. Neither am I.

Keeping these facts straight is essential to doing life better and being a person of wisdom. It's impossible to go smart without having a firm grasp of reality, and that includes understanding the nature of man, the sovereignty of God, and the rightful role of government.

Let's start with humanity: that's you, me, and every other person ever born. The Bible plainly declares that we come forth from the womb with an inclination to selfishness and pride, what theologians call "concupiscence." Our eyes, ears, and experience should convince us of the same thing. We don't have to teach little children to lie, to be selfish, to cheat, or to hit. The nightly newscast is little more than a recital of the horrors and abuses human beings have inflicted upon one another in the preceding twenty-four hours.

Nevertheless, many people deny that we are (if I may quote Lady Gaga again) "born that way." If, contrary to what the Bible teaches, people are born basically good, then there must be some other explanation for the sin we see all around us. Why do people hoard wealth while others starve? Why else do they steal, cheat, rape, molest, and kill? Why do we all lie, lust, and covet—every last one of us? If the problem isn't *internal* to man, it must be *external*.

When an atrocity like the Charleston church massacre takes place, those who deny that we're all born with an innate propensity to do evil start grasping for an external cause—"We have too many guns" being their favorite. They blame the inanimate object. "Take away the gun and you solve the puzzle," goes the argument, but it doesn't hold water. Think about it. That's like blaming the pencil for the misspelled word. A man with murder in his heart doesn't need a gun; a moving car, a knife, a hammer, or even a rock will do the job. The Bible says the human heart, untouched by God's redemptive love and grace, is more deceptive than we can comprehend, capable of more evil than we want to admit. Guns are not the problem. I think it's fair to debate if the mentally ill should have access to guns, but even then, if someone has a heart to do bad things, he can find a way to do it. The same is true of money, a morally neutral tool that can be used for evil or good, to help the poor or to buy drugs. Whether money becomes an instrument for good or evil depends on the heart of the person who uses it.

Because every one of us is born with concupiscence—bent the wrong way, as it were—the Christian community speaks of being "born again." We need a second birth that addresses the twisted root of what makes us what we are. Otherwise we're only dealing with symptoms. If you want to remove weeds from your garden, you have to dig them up at the root. Some people simply don't want to look at the root of what makes us what we are—good or bad—so they're constantly searching for external solutions to the internal problem.

This brings us to government. We can pass a law that makes it illegal for me to hurt someone else, but that law can't help me deal with what's going on inside of me. Policies and programs can't fix my human brokenness. Believing the government can and should solve every problem goes hand in hand with the false belief that the root of mankind's problems is external rather than internal.

There is a God-ordained place for government power. The Bible makes that clear. There is also a messianic impulse in those who think every problem of society requires a government policy or program. It's a religious impulse that requires a type of *faith*. I say faith because the overwhelming evidence is that government programs rarely make problems better and frequently make worse the very ills they were crafted to address. In other words, the "big government" advocates walk by faith, not by sight.

Christians look to God's Son, Jesus Christ, as the Messiah—that is, the ultimate source of security, life, meaning, and happiness. Liberalism, however, looks to the state for those blessings. It's a form of idolatry, chasing a false messiah. As Pastor Jimmy Evans says, "The bigger your government, the smaller your God. The smaller your government, the bigger your God."

The danger of investing too much power in the government is that the ranks of government, on both the elected and bureaucratic sides, are filled with people who are just as broken, twisted, and flawed as everyone else. Power corrupts. The temptations of greed, graft, corruption, self-promotion, and power-grabbing in Washington are overwhelming.

I witnessed these things with my own eyes. Good men and women, moved by noble principles, arrive brimming with good intentions. Within a few years, they get sucked into the power-brokering machine, and far too often those intentions are displaced by uglier motivations as they learn to play the "Beltway game." A fellow once told me during my time in Congress, "You guys come to Washington thinking it's a cesspool and after six months you think it's a Jacuzzi."

This happens on both sides of the political aisle. Both parties have powerful, deep-pocketed special interest groups that look to them to manipulate the levers of public policy to their advantage. But occasionally a politician arrives in Washington who refuses to play the game.

Texas Republican Jeb Hensarling sent shock waves through the U.S. Chamber of Commerce, the giant multinational corporations, and Wall Street's titans of finance when he announced, "I'm not pro-business. I'm pro–free enterprise," meaning he was more concerned about businesses' competing for the customer than he was in protecting a company's deal.

If I sell reading glasses for two dollars a pair, someone should have the right to set up shop next to me and sell them for $1.50 a pair. That's free enterprise. But if the government prevents my competitor from doing that, it's protecting my deal. Jeb's not for protecting anyone's deal. Another way to kill competition is to pile up burdens on businesses—regulations, taxes, a litigious environment—that the big guys can handle but little guys can't. Free enterprise has plenty of enemies, and they're not all in the government or the Democratic Party.

This is precisely why the founding fathers limited the reach of the national government. The framers of the Constitution may not all have been born-again Christians, but they shared the biblical view of mankind as fallen and easily corruptible. Those constitutional restraints, unfortunately, have been eroded in recent years by activist courts, a passive Congress, and an over-reaching executive branch.

So if government programs—prone as they are to inefficiency, waste, corruption, and abuse—aren't the solution, what is the answer for poverty, racism, injustice, and the rest of society's ills? God's design has always been for His people—the church—to be that answer, but we have largely neglected that redemptive role in our society. In our preoccupation with the sweet by and by we have neglected the gritty here and now. In our obsession with outward behavior, we have ignored sins of the heart. Our Gospel message needs to be one of both personal righteousness and social justice.

For example, we rightly preach against sexual sin, yet rarely do we rail against what happens to inmates after their release from prison. Pornography is a terrible destroyer of human souls, but so is greed. Rarely do we hear sermons concerning racism. How can I say I hate my white, black, red, yellow, or brown brother when he is made in the image of God just as I am? We have, at best, paid lip service to the plight of the poor in our own communities. Sadly, the church has lost some of its influence in the world because it preaches individual rectitude and ignores justice.

I'm not advocating the redistribution of wealth through the coercive arm of the government. That's nothing more than being generous with someone else's money. I'm suggesting that we, God's people, offer compassion, concern, and meaningful help to those who are struggling. I don't want to punish those who have much, but I don't want to forget about those who have little. Is it too much to ask that we make an effort to understand what people who don't look like us have been through historically in the hope of better understanding why they're struggling today? Is it too much to reach out and help them build a better future? When I see people who are struggling, selfish, failing, addicted to alcohol or drugs, incarcerated, their marriages falling apart, I see myself apart from the grace of God. The answer to poverty and injustice is the church being the church, not the government being the government.

If we want to transform society, we have to be transparent. We often encourage a warped view of Christianity because we love talking about the glorious parts of our salvation but rarely reveal the broken, dysfunctional parts of our lives that have been touched and redeemed by the grace of Christ. We appear to have it together and to have always had it together, as if somehow that required less of God's mercy than other people. We mustn't let spiritual pride be an obstacle to the transformation that the true Gospel can bring to whole segments of our culture.

When we're transparent about all the mess God has brought us through and delivered us from, people in a mess themselves feel hopeful instead of judged.

SOME FINAL THOUGHTS ON LIVING A LIFE OF WISDOM

The summer of 1974 had barely begun, but the temperatures were already peaking in the nineties in humid eastern Oklahoma. I had just finished my sophomore year of high school, and the pop radio stations in Tulsa were playing the Stylistics, George McCrae, and Gladys Knight.

One afternoon, I was in the middle of the third item on the list of chores my father had assigned me for that day—mowing our lawn—when an unfamiliar car rolled up in front of our house. A white, middle-aged gentleman stepped out, placed a Stetson cowboy hat on his head, and started walking in my direction.

I cut the mower engine, curious about this mysterious stranger, wondering what he was doing in my neighborhood. He introduced himself as Mr. Ben Carroll and said he was the area superintendent for the Army Corps of Engineers. I knew the corps administered nearby Eufaula Lake, the huge man-made reservoir that took its name from my hometown.

"I'd like to hire two black kids for the summer," he told me as I wiped the sweat out of my eyes with my t-shirt. "Do you know anyone who might be interested?"

Well, I knew one black kid who was certainly interested. The prospect of getting *paid* for work instead of laboring through my family chores every day merely for room and board was powerfully appealing. I signed up on the spot and referred a buddy of mine as well. We worked hard that summer, made decent money, and gained valuable experience in the world of work.

I was grateful for the job at the time. Later, as I learned more about how the world works, I gained a deeper appreciation for what Mr. Carroll did that day. He had a limited number of jobs for young people in the area, and he crossed the railroad tracks because he wanted to make sure a couple of guys who looked like me got a shot at them. He wasn't required to meet some quota. He chose to do it because it was the decent thing to do. Neither he nor I had any idea he was offering a job to a future member of Congress who would have a say in the corps' policies. He went out of his way to provide opportunity to someone with initiative and a willingness to work hard. I've never forgotten that.

That's all a lot of people need: the opportunity to build some confidence and momentum. One thing leads to another. They just need a start and sometimes a second chance. How much better would our nation be if every employer would catch the spirit of that corps superintendent?

I'm so grateful for the opportunities I've been given over the years. I'm also glad God doesn't require perfection on our part before He'll use us, because there are no perfect people. It's encouraging that the Bible is filled with flawed, imperfect people—many with huge mistakes on their resumes—who went on to be used mightily by God. Some changed the course of history.

Noah couldn't handle his liquor. Moses murdered a man. David was an adulterer who contracted a killing to cover his sin. Jonah ran from God. These folks had short-comings. Some were utterly dysfunctional. But because of God's grace they were used in powerful ways.

If God required perfect vessels, He would have no one on earth to use. As I've said, I'm the most perfectly imper-fect person you will ever meet, but I've consistently grown as a person and found myself used by God. Why is that? For one thing, I've never considered my imperfections and dysfunctions as my "normal." I've never looked at that ver-sion of myself and shrugged saying, "That's just the way I am."

Yes, God loves us just as we are, but he refuses to leave us as we are. I'm so glad I didn't have to clean myself up to come to God. He always meets me right where I am. I'm even happier that He then leads me to a better place.

God wants us to learn to do life better today than we did it yesterday. Better this month than last month. Better this year than last year. God's wisdom book, Proverbs, compares this upward progress to the gradual breaking of day: "But the path of the righteous is like the light of dawn that shines brighter and brighter until the full day."

These natural eyes of mine may be getting a little dimmer with the years, but my spiritual eyes have never seen this truth more clearly. Giving God control of your life is the wisest thing you can do. A life placed in His hands is like wet clay. The more it yields to His direction, the more aligned it is with His wisdom principles, the more pliable is that clay. He is an extraordinary artist. Again and again I've seen Him take the most misshaped and twisted of lives and turn them into beautiful masterpieces. The Apostle Paul surely had God's patient artistry in mind when He wrote to some friends, "For I am confident of this very thing, that He who began a good work in you will perfect it until the day of Christ Jesus."[19]

By no means is a life with God a trouble-free journey. We're still living in a broken world filled with broken people. Life happens. Heartaches, setbacks, injustices, and disappointments will come. Yet God is aware of them all and walks with us through every valley, ever propelling us to the mountaintops. That's the truth I want to explore in greater depth on the pages ahead.

CHAPTER 7

STAND ON BROAD SHOULDERS

If I have seen further, it is by standing on the shoulders of giants.

—Sir Isaac Newton

The opening twenty-five minutes of the film *Saving Private Ryan* may be some of the most intense and gut wrenching in cinematic history. In 1998, Steven Spielberg put ordinary civilians directly inside the chaos and terror of war in a way that many combat veterans confirmed was spot-on and authentic. But when I evaluate my life, it's the end of that movie, not the beginning, that comes to mind.

The "Private Ryan" who needs saving is young James Francis Ryan, the lone survivor among four brothers serving in World II. His three brothers were all killed in action on the same day, two in the D-Day invasion at Normandy and one in the South Pacific. In hopes of keeping Mother Ryan from losing her last boy, Captain John Miller leads a squad of battle-weary Rangers into German-occupied France to retrieve him. Enduring hardship, danger, and loss, Miller remarks, "This Ryan better be worth it."

After eventually finding Ryan, the squad is forced to make a stand against a German advance so Ryan can escape to Allied lines. Shot and dying, Miller grabs the young man by his jacket and pleads, "James…earn this. *Earn it.*"

That scene resonates so powerfully with me because I identify with Private Ryan. I know beyond any doubt that the productive and rewarding life I've been privileged to live so far was made possible by the heavy sacrifices of some who went before me. I'm keenly aware that the wide paths I've walked were once unmarked trails that had to be hacked out of a wilderness of resistance by great and courageous souls. In other words, I am mindful that I behold these vistas because I'm standing on the shoulders of giants.

There is no such thing as a "self-made" person. As I look back across the years at those who sowed wisdom, meaning, and encouragement in my life, I'm struck by their diversity. I see black, white, and Native American faces who inspired me to dig deep and work to become a better version of myself, some of whom I never personally met, but upon whose broad shoulders I, and many others, nevertheless stand.

EUFAULA ROOTS

Not surprisingly, the two people most responsible for my faith, character, and values are Buddy and Helen Watts, my parents. Their efforts were augmented by a proud uncle named Wade, who served as state president of the NAACP for years in Oklahoma, and a proud grandmother named Mittie. From my father I received a rich inheritance, but one not measured in dollars or acres. He gave his children an *example*. My brother Lawrence calls it "the Buddy Watts anointing." He modeled a monumental work ethic and made sure it was passed on to us. If you're over fifty, regardless of your color, you know exactly what I'm talking about, because your parents did the same thing.

I cannot recall a time when I was growing up that my father wasn't holding down at least three jobs. He took his responsibility as provider for his tribe more seriously than words can express. He usually worked sixteen-to-eighteen-hour days as a policeman, a farmer, and an entrepreneur. Oh, and he also preached on Sundays! It took a toll on him, but he didn't complain. Later in his life, an EKG revealed that at some point he'd suffered a mild heart attack and just kept going. As we used to say in football, he "walked it off." That's how tough he was.

When I looked around my neighborhood as a boy, I saw men working. The expectation of hard work was in the air like oxygen. My mother worked long and hard each day as well. The same was true of us children—Melvin, Lawrence, Mildred, Gwen, and Darlene. It never occurred to us to complain, because we didn't know there was any other way to live. And this experience wasn't unique to my family. That's just the way it was for us and every other family—the Selmons, the McNeals, the Joneses, the Pierces, the Batsons, the Moores. Whatever your name, you understood the importance of hitching up to the wagon and helping to pull it.

In addition to my chores at home, I helped my grandmother whenever she needed me. I would be dispatched to mow her lawn (with her old manual mower), dig worms so she could go fishing, or do whatever she needed. Now most of the time when I arrived at her house, she had work for me to do, but sometimes she would have a five-dollar bill for me instead of a job. A shrewd motivator, Mittie knew how to make sure that Junior—that's what she called me—was always eager to make himself available. And I was! Five dollars was a princely sum for a kid back when ten cents would buy a big candy bar and fifteen cents would secure a sixteen-ounce bottle of pop—sixteen cents with the penny tax!

When I think about my mother, I recall her many home remedies and therapies. Visits to the doctor, an expensive luxury, were a last resort in the Watts household. If no bones were broken, my mother relied on various Watkins or Raleigh products and a combination of liniments, oils, and salts, nursing us with the methods that had been passed down from generation to generation.

Without the sacrifice, teaching, and example of Buddy and Helen Watts, nothing that I've done or become would have been possible. Because of them, I've gone farther than anyone would have dreamed a kid from the other side of the tracks in the hills of Oklahoma could go.

COACHES AND MENTORS

Can a junior high basketball coach change a life? One changed mine. His name is Bruce Shropshire.

I was in eighth grade and had just made an embarrassing and costly error in a game against our despised archrivals, Checotah. Grabbing a defensive rebound but forgetting which end of the court we were on, I put a shot back up. That's right—in a game we wanted to win more than any other, I scored a goal for the enemy!

A minute later, a teammate of mine recovered a loose ball and started dribbling toward the wrong goal. Shouts from the bench and the stands turned him around before it was too late, but this was the last straw for Coach Shropshire. "Anyone who doesn't know which basket is ours shouldn't be out on the floor," he yelled after the game. His frustration was understandable, but it added an extra dose of humiliation to the heaping helping already served up to the two Wrong Way Corrigans. The next day, we stewed about the episode together, stoking each other's anger and eventually talking ourselves into quitting the team. When we told Coach Shropshire, he dismissed my friend but asked me to stay behind. Seeing my potential and refusing to let me quit, he said I was making a mistake that might follow me for the rest of my life and he refused to accept my uniform. He was right.

Paul Bell, my high school football coach, Perry Anderson, my high school basketball coach, and their assistants, Robert Newton and Lamar Armstong, were all old school. No excuses. They taught "team first" and "earn it." Coach Newton thought I was a show-off because I wore white shoes when everyone else was wearing black shoes. I just thought white shoes looked better, and sure enough, before the season was over, most of our players were in white shoes.

If it weren't for these coaches, I might never have been recruited by the University of Oklahoma. I learned so much from many good people there, but three men stand out.

The first is Barry Switzer. He taught me about confidence, the importance in being comfortable in your own skin, and dealing with adversity. Thank heavens we didn't lose much, but when we did, Coach Switzer would always remind us to be good losers. He wasn't saying accept it or like it. He was saying to be a man about it.

The second is Galen Hall, our quarterback coach. He didn't say a lot, but when he did speak, it meant something, and he had an uncanny ability to know when my mind was wandering. After a bad play, he'd bark, "J. C., bear down!" By *bear down* he meant focus, concentrate—in other words, dig deep. To this day, when stress, chaos, or distraction threatens to pull me off course, I think of Coach Hall's exhortation, and I say to myself, "J. C., bear down."

The third outstanding influence on me at OU was the academic advisor for scholarship athletes, a Sooner legend named Port Robertson. If you played at OU while Port was there, just reading his name will conjure up fear and admiration. Robertson had coached the Sooner wrestling team to three NCAA titles and the U.S. Olympic freestyle wrestling team to three gold medals in eight weight classes in Rome, one of the best showings for the United States in Olympic wrestling history. He also coached the freshman football squad during the Bud Wilkinson era, playing a major role in shaping the Sooner football program in a career that spanned portions of five decades.

Prior to arriving in Norman, Robertson served a five-and-a-half-year stint in the army during World War II. Remember the landing on Omaha Beach depicted in *Saving Private Ryan*? Port was there, earning a Purple Heart and the Bronze Star, eventually leaving the service with the rank of captain. That tough, no-nonsense military background came through in his dealings with young athletes like me. As one chronicler of OU's history has written, "No person in the University of Oklahoma athletics department was more respected or feared than Port Robertson."[1]

Robertson's job was to see to it that the "peaheads," as he called us athletes, attended class, showed up at study hall, and did all the things necessary to graduate, an assignment that he pursued as if the orders had come from General Eisenhower himself.

If you were late for study hall, missed a class, or committed some other peaheaded infraction, you might have your plate broken, meaning you couldn't eat in the chow hall, or be assigned to a tour of duty in the cafeteria beginning at six o'clock in the morning. Skipping a class could mean running the ninety-six steps of Memorial Stadium's lower level. A former OU wrestler recalls that the first time Port sentenced him to running stadium steps, he asked, "How many sets, Coach?" Port answered, "Nine and a half." To the wrestler's puzzled look, Port responded, "Peahead, I don't really care how you get down after the last trip up."

I vividly recall one of the first times I encountered Robertson. Like a drill sergeant addressing a batch of green recruits, he let us know in no uncertain terms how things were going to be: "You peaheads will follow my rules. There will be no excuses. There will be no mercy. And most importantly of all, gentlemen, there will be no thongs worn into my office." Today we call them flip-flops, but whatever they're called, Robertson despised them. One day my team-mate Steve Rhodes and I were called into Robertson's office, and Steve unthinkingly waltzed in there wearing his flip-flops. When Port saw them his face was calm. He politely got out of his chair, walked around his desk, and stood on top of Steve's feet. Then he started twisting with all his weight. He said, "You little peahead, you know how I feel about those things." I doubt Steve ever made that mistake again.

White, black, Native American, Hispanic, he treated us all the same—with a character-building rod of iron.

After a while we began to understand that beneath that drill sergeant demeanor beat a heart that genuinely cared for the young men who came under his watchful eye. Occasionally he would let evidence of that affection slip out. One time when I ran afoul of Robertson's Rules, he called me into his office and said, "Peahead, how do you think you're going to remain one of my favorite people making decisions like that?"

Every athlete who went through the University of Oklahoma in that era has his own Port Robertson stories. One rainy evening in my freshman year, we were due at study hall. We stood at the doorway of our dorm looking at the rain and contemplating the ten-minute walk across campus. Darrel Ray, Terry Jones, John Goodman, Freddie Nixon, Steve Rhodes, and I discussed the matter and decided not to go. "It's raining pretty hard," we reasoned. "Port will understand." The rain let up considerably a few minutes later, however, and we thought better of our plan to skip, making a dash for study hall but arriving seven minutes late. Needless to say we got reported to Port for being late.

He was not pleased. When we offered our rain excuse, Port squinted at us for a moment then said, "Peaheads, the next time you're wondering whether or not it's raining too hard for you to run to study hall, here's what I want you to do. If you're ever in doubt, I want you to take a cup and carry it with you as you run to study hall. If your cup is full when you get here, then yes, it was probably raining too hard for you to go." We got the message.

Port Robertson's style of motivation and discipline is now a relic of the past. There are too many trial lawyers looking for a case and too many reporters looking for a story for such tactics to be used today. Even if it were possible, I suspect too few young men today possess the mental toughness to respond to that kind of discipline and training thanks to the twin epidemics of fatherlessness and divorce. God created both mothers and fathers, giving them crucial but distinct roles in guiding children to adulthood. Mothers are generally predisposed to nurture and comfort. Fathers— as God originally envisioned them—instill toughness and resilience, among other character traits. As Pastor Robert Morris observes, "When a child falls and scrapes his or her knee, the mother's role is to clean it, bandage it, and kiss it. The father's role is to then say, 'Okay, you're going to live. Now stop crying and get back out there and play.'" Have we produced a generation of young adults who have received lots of mothering but very little fathering?

With age and wisdom, I've come to appreciate what Port did for me and for hundreds of other young men. Nineteen-year-olds generally have no sense of the future, they are too young to know what they don't know, falsely believe they're immortal, tend to think rules are for other people, and have little capacity to endure short-term pain for long-term gain. Port Robertson's clear boundaries and expectations, enforced with fierce accountability, were exactly what I needed in that season of my life.

Several years after he retired, I ran into Port at a local gas station. I was serving in Congress and was widely viewed as an up-and-comer on the political scene. At one point in our conversation, he paused, gave me that familiar soul-penetrating stare right in the eyes, and then said, "J. C. Watts, I'm pretty proud of you." Those words were like an Olympic gold medal being hung around my neck. I don't know if they would have meant any more if my own father had uttered them. I thank God for Port Robertson.

A mentor has been defined as "a brain to pick, an ear to listen, and a push in the right direction."[2] When I tossed my hat into the political ring for the first time, a wise Native American woman with silver-streaked hair became such a mentor to me. Helen TeAta Cole, half Chickasaw and half Choctaw, was born in 1922. Her middle name was given in honor of her famous aunt, TeAta Fisher, a world-renowned Chickasaw storyteller. I loved to hear Helen talk about her aunt.

Helen had been a trailblazer in Oklahoma herself, elected to the Oklahoma House of Representatives in 1978 and then to the state Senate in 1984. She was still serving in the Senate when she first took me under her wing. Over the next few years she invested, encouraged, corrected, and confronted with equal parts love, wisdom, and candor.

At the height of my Corporation Commission ordeal, when I was being pummeled in the press, I went to Helen for counsel and consolation, and she told me a story that completely changed my perspective. At a time when Helen herself was being lied about in the press, she asked an experienced mentor, "Do you ever get used to this?" He replied, "No, you don't ever get used to it, but you can make peace with the fact that it is the price you have to pay to make a difference."

It was advice Port Robertson would have appreciated. In her own gracious way, Helen was saying, "Toughen up! If changing the world were easy, everyone would be doing it." I never forgot that wisdom, and it served me well in the years that followed. Helen would have made a great coach.

Helen was fond of calling me a "son," and I was proud to have such a great woman think of me that way. She's gone now, but as I write, her actual son, Tom Cole, holds the congressional seat that I once held. Tom and I are both beneficiaries of her great wisdom and both a part of her legacy.

THE BROADEST OF SHOULDERS

On more than one occasion as I walked the halls of Congress, I recalled that Abraham Lincoln had walked those same corridors, treading upon the same marble tiles. In moments like that, I am moved with gratitude for Lincoln's courage and convictions. "I pledge my life and my party to the fact that all men are created equal," he proclaimed. I've often reminded my Republican friends who think Christians should hold their tongue about social issues that the Republicans of Lincoln's day thought he was talking too much about freeing the slaves—a social issue. If he had followed their advice, no one would have heard of J. C. Watts. I stand on Lincoln's shoulders.

I've also found great inspiration in the lives of men like Frederick Douglass and Booker T. Washington. Examining their lives makes me keenly aware that any brushes with racism or discrimination I've experienced along the way were nothing compared to what those who went before me endured.

A former slave who worked tirelessly in the cause of abolition, Douglass was one of the great minds and orators of the nineteenth century. For his relentless efforts to keep the cause of equality before the president, he has variously been called "Lincoln's conscience" and "Lincoln's thorn." Lincoln himself called him simply a "friend."[3]

Booker T. Washington rightly saw that the most effective pathway to enduring equality for black Americans was economic empowerment rather than politics. He advocated education, entrepreneurship, self-improvement, and self-reliance as the foundations for the advancement of black people. He believed that political power follows economic power, while the reverse is not necessarily true. His counsel was largely ignored by several generations of civil rights leaders and, sadly, history has validated Washington's warnings.

Even so, as a business owner, entrepreneur, and advocate for small business, I like to think that I and many others I know represent what Washington hoped to see happen in the black community. "Character," he said, "not circumstances, makes the man."[4] And he urged his students at the famed Tuskegee Institute, "There is no power on earth that can neutralize the influence of a high, pure, simple and useful life."[5] These are the very themes I've attempted to advance in this book.

Of course, I could not compile such a list of broad-shouldered forerunners without mentioning the titanic contribution of the Reverend Martin Luther King. I doubt there is any African American male over fifty years of age who wasn't profoundly affected by Dr. King. I certainly was. He didn't just preach non-violence and courage in the face of injustice. He lived them. In fact, he exemplified them.

I never saw my father cry. Yet on the night of April 4, 1968, I saw him cover his eyes and run into his bedroom so his children wouldn't see him weeping in grief at the news that Dr. King had been assassinated. At the age of ten, I couldn't grasp all that was happening, but I knew something profound and awful had taken place. The champion of non-violence had fallen victim to violence. The man who refused to hate had been cut down by hate.

Dr. King has been gone a long time now, but his wisdom and character continue to inspire. To this day I am challenged, reproved, and inspired by words such as these: "An individual has not started living fully until they can rise above the narrow confines of individualistic concerns to the broader concerns of humanity. Every person must decide at some point, whether they will walk in light of creative altruism or in the darkness of destructive selfishness. This is the judgment: Life's most persistent and urgent question is: 'What are you doing for others?'"[6]

THE LIFE OF PRENTICE GAUTT

When I strolled onto the picturesque campus of the University of Oklahoma in the fall of 1976 with a football scholarship in my pocket, I was one of roughly eight hundred black students enrolled at that time. When I showed up at my first football practice, I saw lots of faces that looked just like mine.

That wouldn't have been the case twenty years earlier. In the fall of 1956, there were only a handful of black students on the entire OU campus. There had never been a black athlete, at least not until Prentice Gautt arrived at the invitation of Coach Bud Wilkinson.

In those days, an invitation from Bud Wilkinson was the next best thing to an invitation from God Himself. By the fall of 1956, his football teams had already won two national championships and would go on to win another that year. The Sooners were in the middle of a history-making forty-seven-game winning streak—they hadn't lost since the third game of 1953—a record no team has ever come close to matching.* For some additional perspective

---

*That streak would come to an end in a 7–0 loss to Notre Dame on November 16, 1957, two days before I was born.

on how successful the Sooners were in the Wilkinson era, consider that they had also run off a thirty-one-game winning streak. Between the second game of the 1948 season and the eighth game of the 1957 season, Wilkinson's teams went 94–4–2.

Gautt had been a standout halfback at Oklahoma City's Douglass High School, a historically all-black school named in honor of Frederick Douglass. Two years earlier, in 1954, the U.S. Supreme Court's decision in *Brown v. Board of Education* had signaled the beginning of the end of school segregation in America, but it would take a number of years for the implications of that decision to be worked out in the nation's segregated school systems. That was certainly the case in Oklahoma City.

For most of Gautt's high school years, black schools played only other black schools, though change was arriving by his senior year, when he played in the first integrated high school football game ever held in Oklahoma and was the first black athlete to appear in the annual All-State game, earning MVP honors. A star in the classroom as well as on the field, Gautt was a member of the National Honor Society and president of his senior class.

Growing up, Gautt had dreamed of nothing else but playing for Bud Wilkinson and wearing the crimson and cream, a desire that stemmed not so much from concern for the cause of racial equality but from watching the Sooners win game after game on his family's little black-and-white television set.

Norman was only twenty miles down the road from Gautt's home, but in 1956 his dream seemed impossibly distant to most of those around him. What's more, major football powers in several Northern states, where the color barrier had been broken several years earlier, were expressing interest in Gautt. With his sterling academic credentials, there was no doubt he could play college football and receive a first-class education at someplace like Michigan or Minnesota. Yet that was not his dream.

When he told his mother he wanted to play at Oklahoma, she tried to steer him toward an easier, safer path, telling him, "Prentice, this is something that you need to think about. In my opinion, you need to go someplace where the roads have already been crossed. The first black man to cross the road is usually the one who gets killed."[7] Prentice couldn't be dissuaded. It was Oklahoma or nothing.

Coach Wilkinson knew great football talent when he saw it. He wanted to offer Gautt a scholarship, but when word of his plans filtered out, the pressure from powerful alumni and skittish administrators grew too intense. Wilkinson would welcome Gautt to his team if he became a student at OU, but there would be no scholarship. This was troubling, for Gautt's family had no money.

When the news that Gautt could play for the Sooners if he attended OU spread through Oklahoma City's black community, a small group of doctors, pharmacists, and community leaders raised funds for a scholarship. It turned out that finding the money to attend the University of Oklahoma was the easy part. Running the daily gauntlet of insults, slurs, wisecracks, and humiliations was the real test. In most classrooms, OU's tiny handful of black students were required to sit in the back row or, in some cases, out in the hallway.

Gautt's fellow players were cautious at first, but he won them over with his incredible work ethic on the field and his profound decency off of it. First, he earned their respect, then he earned their loyalty and affection. In fact, his teammates ultimately stood with Prentice to hammer away at some of the vestiges of Jim Crow. Jakie Sandifer from Texas—a prince of a man whom I was privileged to count as a dear friend before he passed away—roomed with Prentice on the road, an act of real courage.

On one occasion, the team bus was scheduled to stop at a diner after a game. Coach Wilkinson prudently called ahead to make sure the establishment would serve a black player. The owner, eager to sell forty or fifty chicken dinners in one sitting, said "Sure, no problem." When the team arrived and was seated, though, the owner wasn't present. When the manager walked out and saw a young black man sitting at the table, he threw a fit. Prentice, all too familiar with this routine, slowly rose to head back to the bus with a quiet request that someone bring something out for him to eat. Just then, several of his teammates looked at each other and said, "Hold on. If Prentice can't eat here then I'm not either." In quick order, the entire team filed out of the restaurant and back onto the bus. They eventually found a place down the road eager to have that much business.

Before the 1957 contest in the Cotton Bowl against the archrival Texas Longhorns, Wilkinson sent his team to a hotel in Fort Worth, wisely isolating them from the riotous celebrations in downtown Dallas that always preceded that game. Having been informed that Gautt would not be allowed to stay in the "whites only" establishment—indeed, it would have been a violation of Texas law for him to do so—the Sooner coaches quietly arranged for Prentice to stay at a hotel on the other side of Fort Worth. They had, however, negotiated permission from the hotel for him to rejoin them for the pregame breakfast the next morning. As the team entered the hotel lobby together, Gautt was quietly escorted out a rear door reserved for busboys and maids to a taxi waiting in the alley. When his teammates discovered this arrangement, they were furious—not just with the hotel but with the entire state of Texas.

At breakfast the following morning, one of the team leaders, senior Jim Lawrence, a six-foot-four-inch right tackle, rose and made an impassioned speech, his eyes filling with tears, reminding the team that Prentice hadn't been allowed to stay with them simply because of the color of his skin. In closing, Lawrence nearly shouted, "That's a shame. Football teams are supposed to stick together!" Across the dining room heads nodded and voices muttered agreement. As the sportswriter Jim Dent describes it: "The Sooners were still buzzing when Wilkinson assembled them minutes before kickoff at the Cotton Bowl: 'Win this one for Prentice Gautt.' He didn't need to say another word. The Sooners almost ran over the coaches and everyone else for that matter, as they roared down the long tunnel toward the playing field, the plight of Prentice Gautt now on their minds."[8]

That afternoon the Sooners beat the Longhorns 21–7.

The scholarship that Prentice had been denied his freshman year was happily offered after his first year. He then turned around and donated the money he'd been given to another black student. In one year's time, he had won most skeptics over with his talent and his character. Even so, Coach Wilkinson received a steady stream of hate mail, especially when it became clear that Prentice, as a junior, was going to be a featured starter. Undercover police worked practices and games for protection.

I believe God always knows whom to choose to be a *first*—a barrier breaker, a forerunner. He knows who has not only the talent but the temperament, resilience, character, and mental toughness to persevere through the birth pangs of change. Jackie Robinson was chosen for those reasons. So was Prentice Gautt.

In his remarkable career at OU, Gautt was a two-time all-conference player, MVP of the 1959 Orange Bowl, and an academic All-American. After seven years in the NFL, Gautt coached football at Missouri while earning a Ph.D. in psychology. He went on to serve as assistant commissioner for the Big Eight Conference and in a similar role in the Big 12 Conference.

It's hard to believe that Prentice Gautt's story didn't play out in some distant, musty era of history. No, he took that courageous, lonely step onto that campus the year before I came into this world. I had the pleasure of meeting and visiting with Prentice on several occasions. Each time, we ended up talking about the current state of Sooner football rather than the events of his past. It just didn't seem like the time or the place. I always came away deeply impressed with his humility, intelligence, and gentle spirit. Now that he's gone, I regret not finding an opportunity to hear more about his experiences and to harvest some words of wisdom. I'm especially sad that I didn't take the opportunity to thank him.

I'll always be grateful that a man like Prentice Gautt knew how to dig deep and summon amazing reserves of will, endurance, and courage, opening up the opportunity I would eventually be given at OU. I endeavor to thank him and the other forerunners and mentors for letting me stand on their broad and steady shoulders in the only way I can: by making the most of the opportunities they gave me and by living a life that would make them proud.

EARN THIS

On a Sunday morning in January 2015, while working out on my treadmill before church, I made the mistake of tuning my television to the Sunday morning political talk shows. The mindless bickering and posturing soured my mood and got me thinking about all the selfishness, greed, anger, and hatred in this world. I was ready to wash my hands of everyone and everything when I decided to switch the channel to ESPN for something non-political.

Instead of the sports fix I was seeking, I encountered tearful announcers breaking the news that their longtime colleague Stuart Scott had just died from a rare form of cancer at the age of forty-nine. The news stunned and saddened me, and it put everything I had previously been angry about in perspective. It reminded me not to lose sight of what's really important, smacking me in the face and shouting, "Life is a fragile and precious gift from God. Be a good steward of that gift!"

If we're fortunate, we get a handful of decades on this planet to make something of what God has given us. We can squander those precious days in an ultimately meaningless quest for honors and pleasure or spend them in service to God and our fellow man, leaving a legacy of changed lives. If we make the latter choice, our days will be filled with purpose and deep joy—even in difficult times.

For me, Stuart Scott's passing, sad as it was, served as a much-needed reminder, here in the "third quarter" of my life, to dig deep and not allow my dysfunctions to become my normal, to show up every day and be conscious of working to do life better.

I hear the voices of Frederick Douglass, Martin Luther King, Prentice Gautt, Buddy and Helen Watts, Wade Watts, Paul Bell, Perry Anderson, Bruce Shropshire, and all the others upon whose shoulders I stand, each of these heroes, mentors, and coaches pointing to his door-opening sacrifice and saying, "J. C., earn this."

Each day I try to do just that. I challenge you to do the same. Dig deep.

NOTES

INTRODUCTION: THE POWER OF DIGGING DEEP

1. Caroline Alexander, "Murdering the Impossible," *National Geographic*, June 2006.

2. Reinhold Messner, *The Crystal Horizon: Everest—The First Solo Ascent* (London: Crowood Press, 1989).

CHAPTER 1: THE ADVERSITY UPGRADE

1. Oklahoma State Constitution, Section IX–17: Oath of office—Additional oath.

2. Ronda Fears, "Anthony Claims Bell Officials Paid Cash Inducements," *Journal Record*, October 3, 1992.

3. Ibid.

4.   Ibid.

5.   *Southwestern Bell Telephone Co. v. Oklahoma Corp. Comm.*, 1994 OK 38. 873 P.2d 1001. 65 OBJ 1340. Case Number: 80579. Decided: 04/13/1994. Supreme Court of Oklahoma.

6.   John Greiner, "Anthony Won't Exonerate His Fellow Commissioners," *Daily Oklahoman*, October 7, 1992.

7.   Ibid.

8.   Ibid.

9.   Ibid.

10. Vandewater, Bob. "Watts Says 'I Was Bait' in Anthony FBI Inquiry $7,000 in Campaign Money Intercepted," *Daily Oklahoman*, June 24, 1993.

11. Psalm 103:6–7, NKJV

12. Genesis 50:20, NIV.

13. B. C. Forbes, "Fact and Comment," *Forbes*, March 3, 1923.

14. Martin Luther King Jr., *The American Dream* (sermon at Ebenezer Baptist Church, Atlanta, Georgia, July 4, 1965.

15. Psalm 27:13–14, NASB.

16. Joyce Meyer on Twitter, https://twitter.com/JoyceMeyer/status/608438501487570944.

17. Johnson Oatman, *Count Your Blessings*, 1897.

18. Ibid.

19. Robert A. Emmons and Michael E. McCullough, "Counting Blessings versus Burdens: An Experimental Investigation of Gratitude and Subjective Well-Being in Daily Life," *Journal of Personality and Social Psychology* 84, no. 2 (2003): 377–89.

20. Amit Amin, "The 31 Benefits of Gratitude You Didn't Know About: How Gratitude Can Change Your Life."

21. John Piper, "Guard Yourself with Gratitude," *Desiring God*, 1897.

22. G. K. Chesterton, "A Grace," *The Collected Works of G. K. Chesterton* (San Francisco: Ignatius Press, 1994), 43.

23. Hebrews 10:36, NKJV.

24. I Corinthians 9:24–26, NLT (New Living Translation).

25. Ted Goodman, ed., *The Forbes Book of Business Quotations* (New York: Blackdog & Leventhal, 1997), 646.

26. NKJV.

27. Jim Valvano, "ESPY Awards Speech," March 4, 1993, V Foundation.

28. Glenn van Ekeren, ed., *Speaker's Sourcebook II* (Englewood Cliffs, N.J.: Prentice Hall, 1994), 199.

CHAPTER 2: DIGGING DEEP TO LET GO

1. Kevin Merida, "Black Stars Rising in GOP; Candidates Challenge Party Stereotypes," *Washington Post*, October 30, 1994, sec. A, 1.

2. New Living Translation.

3. Mark 11:25–26 NKJV.

4. NKJV.

5. Matthew 18:23–35.

6. Charles R. Swindoll, *Improving Your Serve* (Nashville: Thomas Nelson, 2004).

7. Thomas Sowell, "Dishonest Political Correctness Harms All," Creator's Syndicate, October 29, 2013.

8. William Voegeli, "The Redskins and Their Offense," *Claremont Review of Books*, XIV, no. 2.

9. Frank Rich, "In Conversation with Chris Rock," Vulture.com.

10. "Some Losses inevitable, but Churches Can Guard the Back Door," Lifeway Research, http://www.lifewayresearch.

com/2006/10/26/some-losses-inevitable-but-churches-can-
guard-the-back-door/.

11. I Samuel 16:7, NKJV.

12. Psalm 139:23–24, NASB.

13. Matthew 7:24–28.

14. "Dolly Parton: Quotes," IMDB.com, http://m.imdb.com/
name/nm0000573/quotes.

15. David W. DeFord, ed., *1000 Brilliant Achievement Quotes:
Advice from the World's Wisest* (Ordinary People Can Win!,
2004), 24.

16. Op. cit. Jack Canfield.

17. Jack Canfield, *The Success Principles: How to Get from
Where You Are to Where You Want to Be* (New York: Collins,
2005).

18. Mark 11:23–26, NASB.

19. Lydia Warren, "'I Forgive You': Tearful Relatives of Charleston
Victims Confront 'Killer' in Court," *Daily Mail*, June 2015,
http://www.dailymail.co.uk/news/article-3131874/Repent-
Relatives-Charleston-killer-s-victims-confront-court-heart-
wrenching-speeches-FORGIVENESS-adopts-vacant-
remorseless-stare.html.

CHAPTER 3: UNLEARN AND RETHINK

1. Scott Plous (1993), *The Psychology of Judgment and Decision
Making*, McGraw-Hill, ISBN 978-0-07-050477-6, OCLC
26931106.

2. Op. cit. Van Ekeren. *Speaker's Sourcebook II*. P.61.

3. Sydney J. Harris, *Pieces of Eight* (Boston: Houghton Mifflin,
1882).

4. Ibid.

5. C. S. Lewis, *Mere Christianity* (London: C. S. Lewis Pte. Ltd., 1952).

6. Proverbs 4:7 KJV.

7. Douglas LaBier, "Are You Suffering from Empathy Deficit Disorder?," *Psychology Today*, April 12, 2010.

8. Ibid.

9. T. D. Jakes, "Thinking Out Loud: A Discourse on Race, Culture, and the Death of Civility," ChristianPost.com.

10. Stephen R. Covey, *The Seven Habits of Highly Effective People* (New York: Free Press, 1989).

11. Isaiah 1:18.

12. Gerald Holton, "Candor in Science", *Synthese*, Vol. 145, No. 2 (June 2005), 179.

13. Romans 12:2 NASB.

14. Caroline Leaf, "Toxic Thoughts," DrLeaf.com, http://drleaf. com/about/toxic-thoughts/.

15. Psalm 139:23–24.

16. II Corinthians 10:5.

17. Tony Evans, "Think On?," TonyEvans.org, http://tonyevans. org/2013/12/think-on/.

18. Jon R. Katzenbach, Ilona Steffen, and Caroline Kronley, "Cultural Change That Sticks," *Harvard Business Review*, July 2012, https://hbr.org/2012/07/cultural-change-that-sticks/ ar/1.

19. Alan Murray, *The Wall Street Journal Essential Guide to Management* (New York: Harper Business, 2010), http:// guides.wsj.com/management/innovation/how-to-change-your-organizations-culture/.

20. Maugham, Somerset. *The Summing Up* (New York: George H. Doran Company, 1919), 223.

21. Mark 7:13.

22. Galatians 3:28, NASB.

23. Martin Luther King Jr., "MLK at Western," Western Michigan University, http://www.wmich.edu/sites/default/files/attachments/MLK.pdf.

24. E. C. Morris, *Sermons, Addresses and Reminiscences and Important Correspondence, With a Picture Gallery of Eminent Ministers and Scholars* (Nashville: National Baptist Publishing Board, 1885).

CHAPTER 4: HISTORY NEED NOT BE DESTINY

1. Rick Warren, *The Purpose Driven Life: What on Earth Am I Here For? Expanded Edition* (Grand Rapids, Mich.: Zondervan, 2012).

2. Roy B. Zuck, ed., *The Speaker's Quote Book* (Grand Rapids, Mich.: Kregel Publications, 1997), 180.

3. Ashyia Henderson, *Contemporary Black Biography* (Gale Research Inc., 2002), 165.

4. John Greenleaf Whittier, *Maud Muller*, stanza 53.

5. Romans 3:10 (NKJV).

6. Joyce Meyer, *Beauty for Ashes: Receiving Emotional Healing* (New York: Warner Faith, 2008).

7. Deborah Hedstrom-Page, *From Telegraph to Light Bulb with Thomas Edison* (Nashville: B&H Publishing Group, 2007).

8. John C. Maxwell, *Talent Is Never Enough: Discover the Choices That Will Take You Beyond Your Talent* (Nashville: Thomas Nelson, 2007), 132.

9. Bob Knight and Bob Hammel, *Knight: My Story* (New York: St. Martin's Griffin, 2003), 21.

10. Vince Lombardi, "Famous Quotes by Vince Lombardi," VinceLombardi.com.

11. Bob Paladino, *Five Key Principles of Corporate Performance Management* (Hoboken, N.J.: John Wiley & Sons, 2011).

12. Victor Goertzel and Mildred G. Goertzel, *Cradles of Eminence* (New York: Little, Brown & Co., 1962).

13. Alan Loy McGinnis, *Confidence: How to Succeed at Being Yourself* (Minneapolis: Augsburg Fortress, 1987), 63.

14. David W. DeFord, *1000 Brilliant Achievement Quotes: Advice from the World's Wisest* (Omaha: Ordinary People Can Win!, 2004), 14.

15. Philippians 3:13–14 (NASB).

CHAPTER 5: DIGGING DEEP FOR SELF-DISCIPLINE

1. Evan Grant, "Josh Hamilton's Battle: From Cocaine Cravings and 26 Tattoos to Faith and Rangers," *Dallas Morning News*, 2008, http://www.dallasnews.com/sports/texas-rangers/headlines/20150416-josh-hamilton-s-battle-from-cocaine-cravings-and-26-tattoos-to-faith-and-rangers.ece.

2. Josh Hamilton and Tim Keown, "I'm Proof that Hope Is Never Lost," *ESPN Magazine*, July 15, 2008.

3. Austin Murphy, "The Oklahoma Kid," *Sports Illustrated*, October 11, 2004.

4. Glenn Van Ekeren, *Speaker's Sourcebook II: Quotes, Stories, & Anecdotes for Every Occasion* (Englewood Cliffs, N.J.: Prentice Hall, 1994), 295.

5. Luke 9:23.

6. Philippians 3:19.

7. Martin H. Manser, ed., *The Westminster Collection of Christian Quotations* (Louisville, KY: Westminster John Knox Press, 2001).

8. Piers Steel, *The Procrastination Equation: How to Stop Putting Things Off and Start Getting Stuff Done* (Toronto: Random House of Canada, 2010), 84–97.

9. Ibid., 98.

10. Gregg Ten Eishof, *I Told Me So: Self Deception and the Christian Life* (Grand Rapids, MI: Wm. B. Eerdmans Publishing, 2009), 1.

11. Steven Pressfield, (2011-04-20), *Do the Work* (Kindle Location 113), AmazonEncore, Kindle Edition.

12. Zig Ziglar, *See You at the Top* (Gretna, LA: Pelican Publishing, 1975), 166.

13. James Boyce, *Nehemiah: Learning to Lead* (Grand Rapids, MI: Baker Books, 2005).

14. Jack Canfield, *The Success Principles* (New York: Collins, 2007), 51.

15. Thomas Goetz, "Harnessing the Power of Feedback Loops," *Wired*, June 19, 2011.

16. Canfield, op. cit., 102.

17. Steven Pressfield, (2011-04-20), *Do the Work* (Kindle Locations 198–203). AmazonEncore. Kindle Edition.

18. Roy B. Zuck, *The Speaker's Quote Book: Over 5,000 Illustrations and Quotations for All Occasions* (Grand Rapids, MI: Kregel Academic, 2009), 170.

19. See Stuart Buck, *Acting White: The Ironic Legacy of Desegregation* (New Haven, CT: Yale University Press, 2010).

20. Stephen Covey, *First Things First: To Live, to Love, to Learn, to Leave a Legacy* (New York: Simon & Schuster, 1994), 103.

21. David W. Deford, ed., *1000 Brilliant Achievement Quotes: Advice from the World's Wisest* (N.p.: Ordinary People Can Win!, 2006), 55.

CHAPTER 6: GO SMART. BE SMART.

1. *I'm Here*, words and music by Brenda Russell, Allee Willis, and Stephen Bray.

2. Proverbs 4:6–8 (TLV).

3. Proverbs 27:6 (NKJV).

4. Cedrick Brown, *Act Like A Man: Woman, Can You Help Me?* (Bloomington, Ind.: Xlibris, 2013), 124.

5. James Moffatt, op. cit., Zuck, *The Speaker's Quote Book: Over 5,000 Illustrations and Quotations for All Occasions*, 344.

6. I Timothy 6:10.

7. Robert Morris, *The Blessed Life: Unlocking the Rewards of Generous Living* (Grand Rapids, MI: Chosen Books, 2014).

8. Richard G. Briley, *Are You Positive: The Secret of Positive Thinkers' Success* (New York: Berkley Publishing, 1988).

9. Stephen Covey, *First Things First: To Live, to Love, to Learn, to Leave a Legacy* (New York: Simon and Schuster, 1995), 88–89.

10. Bill Hybels, *Simplify: Unclutter Your Soul* (Carol Stream, IL: Tyndale House, 2014).

11. Sarah P. Bailey, "Sweeping away the clutter: A Q&A with Bill Hybels on 'Simplify,'" Religion News Service, http://www.

religionnews.com/2014/08/14/sweeping-away-clutter-qa-bill-hybels-simplify/.

12. Ephesians 5:15, 16 (NLT).

13. Arnold Bennett, *Delphi Collected Works of Arnold Bennett (Illustrated)*, Vol. 1 (N.p.: Delphi Classics, 2013), 4 vols. Print.

14. Selwyn Raab, "Donovan Cleared of Fraud Charges by Jury in Bronx," *New York Times*, May 28, 1987.

15. Psalm 25:7.

16. Proverbs 22:1 (NASB).

17. Alan Ebert, "The Healing of Anita Baker," *Essence*, December 1, 1994.

18. Ephesians 6:7 (NLT).

19. Philippians 4:6 (NASB).

CHAPTER 7: STAND ON BROAD SHOULDERS

1. Jay C. Upchurch, *Tales from the Sooner Sidelines* (N.p.: Sports Publishing, LLC, 2003), 55.

2. S. M. Paul Khurana and P. K. Singhal, eds., *Higher Education: Quality and Management* (New Delhi: Gyan Publishing House, 2010), 154.

3. "When police tried to prevent former slave Frederick Douglass from attending the inaugural reception in 1865, President Lincoln went to the door and said, 'Here comes my friend Douglass!'" William Safire, *Lend Me Your Ears: Great Speeches in History* (New York: W. W. Norton and Co.), 179.

4. Booker T. Washington, "Democracy and Education," Institute of Arts and Sciences. Brooklyn, N.Y., September 30, 1896.

5. Booker T. Washington, *Character Building: Being Addresses Delivered on Sunday Evenings to the Students of Tuskegee Institute* (New York: Doubleday Page & Co, 1902), 144.

6. Coretta Scott King, *The Words of Martin Luther King, Jr.*, Second Edition (2011), 3.

7. Jim Dent, *The Undefeated: The Oklahoma Sooners and the Greatest Winning Streak in College Football* (New York: St. Martin's Press, 2001), 158.

8. Ibid., op cit.